W.K.B{arllen.

S. Thad's.

Far Headingly.

12 X 66

First published 1966

COPYRIGHT © 1966 D. E. JENKINS

London: Lutterworth Press, 4 Bouverie Street, E.C.4.

Philadelphia: Westminster Press, Witherspoon Building,
Philadelphia 7, U.S.A.

Printed in Great Britain by
Page Bros. (Norwich) Ltd., Mile Cross Lane, Norwich

GUIDE
TO THE
DEBATE ABOUT GOD

DAVID E. JENKINS
Fellow and Chaplain, The Queen's College, Oxford

LUTTERWORTH PRESS
LONDON

CONTENTS

INTRODUCTION

DRAMATIS PERSONAE

In this book, the debate about God is traced through the thought of various people whose thought has been influential. The following are the people concerned. The discussion of the book is intended to show why they have been chosen. The brief notes that follow here are simply to assist in 'placing' the thinkers we are to consider.

JOSEPH BUTLER (1692-1752)—Died as Bishop of Durham. Gained fame for his writings on morality and in defence of the Christian conception of the world. See especially his *Sermons at the Rolls* (from 1718 to 1726 he was preacher at the Rolls Chapel) and his *Analogy of Religion.*

FRIEDRICH DANIEL ERNST SCHLEIERMACHER (1768-1834)—A German theologian who had immense influence in Protestant theology in the nineteenth century. He was ordained in 1794 and rapidly became famous as a preacher and writer who could gain a hearing from educated men dominated by the then current rationalism or tired of the formalism of Protestant orthodoxy. He became a Professor of Theology and was for many years Dean of the Faculty of Theology in the then newly-founded University of Berlin. His *Reden über die religion* (English translation, *Religion, Speeches to its Cultured Despisers*—cited in chapter two of this book from John Oman's translation of 1893, republished as a Harper Torch Book in 1958) of 1799 created a sensation, and his great work of *Systematic Theology*, first published in 1821-2, set the tone of Protestant theology for nearly one hundred years.

RUDOLF BULTMANN (b. 1884)—A German New Testament scholar and theologian who was Professor of New Testament Studies at Marburg from 1921 to 1951. Has for many years been a centre of both controversy and inspiration concerning the understanding and interpretation of both the New Testament in particular and the Christian faith in general.

KARL BARTH (b. 1886)—Son of a Professor of New Testament Theology at Berne, he became a pastor in 1909. In 1919 he published a *Commentary on Romans* which marked a radical break from the prevailing theology handed on from the nineteenth century and which seemed to many to speak with extraordinary power and relevance to the grim post-war situation. From 1921 he held professorial posts in Germany until he was expelled in 1935 for his part in leading Church resistance to the Nazis. Since then he has been a Professor at Basle. A prolific and powerful thinker and writer who has won a very considerable following among Protestants and deep respect among Catholic theologians.

EMIL BRUNNER (b. 1889)—A Swiss pastor who taught theology at Zürich from 1922 to 1938 and at Princeton from 1938. Originally one of Karl Barth's foremost supporters in the reaction against nineteenth century theology he had a famous quarrel with him in 1934. Has written many works of systematic theology of which some, such as *The Mediator* and *The Divine Imperative*, have had considerable influence among Anglo-Saxon as well as continental theologians.

PAUL TILLICH (b. 1886)—The son of a Lutheran pastor, he was an army chaplain in the first world war and afterwards became a Professor of Theology and then of Philosophy. He was compelled to leave Germany in 1933 and settled in the U.S.A. where he became Professor of Philosophical Theology at the Union Theological Seminary, New York. He has written extensively on Theology, Philosophy, Religion, History and Culture, and has a very considerable following, particularly in the U.S.A.

DIETRICH BONHOEFFER (1906-1945)—After a brilliant student career at Berlin University and a brief pastorate in Barcelona he taught in Berlin until forbidden by the Nazi authorities in 1936. Had many contacts with and some visits to Great Britain and America and was prominent in the struggle of the Confessing Church in Germany against the Nazi attempt to dictate to German Christians. Chose to return from the U.S.A. to Germany on the eve of the war and became actively concerned in the German resistance movement. Arrested in 1943 and executed in 1945. His *Letters and Papers from Prison* have become famous but he wrote several other influential works of which *The Cost of Discipleship* is probably the title most typical of his life.

Chapter One

THE BEGINNING OF 'THE END OF THEISM'?

THERE HAS ALWAYS been a debate about God, not only about
what He is like, but about whether He exists at all. One conclusion
that it might seem reasonable to draw from this is that there can
be no God. For it might be supposed that God, if He existed,
would be bound to have an existence so certain and so really real
that anyone who was capable of thinking about Him at all would
be bound to see that He really existed. But whatever might be
right to say about God, it is quite clear that many men have
wondered whether He exists at all. Perhaps therefore the simplest
conclusion is that He does not exist. What we have to reckon
with is the fact that many men for much of the time have talked
as if there were a God. But now we know that talk does not
necessarily have to refer to anything beyond itself and so the
simplest and most reasonable conclusion is to stop talking about
God; and that would be the end of the debate.

On the other hand, it might be said that the reasonable conclusion to draw, not only from the quantity but also more
especially from the quality of much of the talk about God, and
from the fact that the debate never seems to come to a final conclusion, is that *of course* God exists. The constant debate about His
existence arises from the fact that God being God, He is infinitely
difficult to talk about, and that man, being not only finite man but
in some sense or other sinful man, finds God not only difficult but
also distasteful to talk about.

However one ought to follow out the types of argument just

touched on, it would seem that the implications of there being a debate about God are themselves debatable. Also, the amount of interest taken in the recent particular public renewal of this debate shows that a sufficient number of people find that this is an issue which they still both want and need to debate. It seems worth while, therefore, to see if we can put our finger on any distinctive features of our current version of this perennial debate. This attempt may help us to decide how we are to assess it. Is it simply a recurring phenomenon which has to be reckoned with as a normal feature of the life of man in the world and of his dealings with and searchings after God? Or does the form which the debate is taking this time show that it is really a decisively heightened crisis of a wasting disease? We want therefore to try and see what is essentially different about this debate and to ask ourselves whether the difference is such that we are reasonably bound to conclude that theism really is on the way out.

This subject is so vast a one and the issues which could reasonably be brought into it can become so complex that we are obliged to seek for some simplifying approach to the whole thing. This book is one man's attempt to offer as clear an account as possible of how he at present is able to make sense of the debate, in the hope that it may be of some assistance to others in making their approach. This is why it has been given the title of *Guide to the Debate about God*. It is offered as an attempt to help people not to feel completely bewildered by the debate, or completely unable to enter into it. To this end, attention will be drawn to what seem to be some of the main questions which are really at issue, and some of the main ways in which it has been found reasonable to go about attempting an answer to these questions. But the most that can be offered, even if the book has some success with some people, is a guide into and a guide in the debate.

It may be felt that to take this approach is to abandon any real hope of believing in God from the start. But in reality the contrary is the case. Whatever may be the happy position of some few believers all of the time, and of most believers some of the time, it is clear that questions about God, including that of His very existence, are debatable in the purely matter of fact sense that people do debate them. And every believer in God knows, at all times as a matter of fact, and sometimes as a matter of fact which is peculiarly pressing upon himself, that a very large number of people today find belief in God difficult or impossible. Now, we may well fear to enter into the debate because we find it too bewildering and complex, so that we are sure that once we enter into it we shall be completely swamped. But to take this attitude is already to have sided with those who do not believe in God.

If God is God, then He is relevant to, and requires to be understood in relation to, everything that is going on and everything that happens to us. As a matter of fact, an intense debate about the existence of God and what it means to believe in Him is going on. Difficulties about believing in God, and doubts about Him assault most of us, and we are surrounded by people who suffer such doubts and difficulties more acutely than ourselves, or else who suffer no such doubts because they are clear that God does *not* exist. For us who believe in God to attempt to keep ourselves aloof from these happenings because we fear that to plunge into them would risk almost certain swamping of our own belief is to assert that for us in practice there is a large and urgent area of thought and life with which we are perforce in contact and yet to which we do not think the God in whom we believe can be related or relevant. This means that we are practical atheists or perhaps, what is worse, really idolaters (but then idolatry is a particularly pernicious form of atheism for idols certainly are no gods, but idol worshippers do not know that they are atheists). To say that we believe in an entity whose scope is not all-embracing would certainly seem to be very similar to giving one's allegiance to some local or tribal deity represented by what the worshippers held to be a suitable idol. Thus to try to keep out of the debate is to admit that for us our God has limited power and scope and so is on a level with other religious idols.

If, on the other hand, we really believe that He is God, we are driven by this belief to enter into the debate and to allow the debate, which is almost certainly within our own hearts and minds, to come out into the open. But if we are to do this as unreservedly, openly and honestly as real belief in a God who is believed to be the true God requires, then we have to face the fact that taking part in a debate is taking part in a debate. That is to say, we have to face the fact that what we need and the most we can look for are guides and helps for entering into and taking part in the debate. If we look for answers that will settle the debate before we are prepared to enter it we are really saying that we refuse to treat the debate as a debate, and that is to say that we will not enter into it. But to say that we will not enter into it is as good as confessing that we do not believe that our God is the true God.

The position, then, from which this book is written is the belief that the God in whom Christians believe is truly God. This belief obliges those who hold it to put it to the utmost test of exposure to, and involvement in, all that is going on in the world and all that happens to each and every one of us. One of the things that is always going on in the world is a debate, on theoretical, practical and emotional levels, about the existence and nature of God. So, for the sake of keeping belief in God alive the debate must be entered into. This means at the present time that believers must fully face the question whether the present debate about God is so critical and distinctive that faith must truly be judged to be on the verge of exposure as an illusion. Just because the debate is a real debate and is about God who must either be relevant to everything or not exist at all, we are bound to find the whole matter singularly bewildering and complex. Hence, we need all the guides and helps that we can get.

One sort of possibly helpful guide is one that attempts to take stock of the particular questions which focus the debate and to arrange them in some coherent order. Such a guide can at best be the temporary pattern which one man has imposed in an over-simplified way on that part of the material with which he has been able to get to grips. Its hoped-for purpose will be to serve as a raft on which one may hope to travel a little further into the midst of the sea of the debate, and also to provide a few sailing directions. As we go on, better means of travel and more comprehensive sailing directions will come to us from our own experience and from the understanding of others. The guide can only be temporary and partial just as experience can only be limited. But the important thing is to set sail. If we hang back we can only face the gradual fading away of whatever belief in God we have, for to hang back is to be disobedient to the implications and imperatives of that belief. But if we launch out into the debate, as we are putting our faith into practice we can only ultimately find our belief being strengthened—if, that is, the God in whom we believe truly is the true God! But that is precisely what the debate is about, and that is what it is the business of faith to allow to be established.

What then is the decisive difference between the debate about God now and the debate between, say, a Platonist and a Sceptic, or a believer and an un-believer in the Middle Ages? The simple answer is—Science. And what, for our purpose, are we to see as the main point about Science? Surely the effect which it has had on our notion of what knowledge is. The question of what knowledge is is one which has exercised the ingenuity and subtlety of thinkers for centuries. And as asking questions about knowledge is thinking about thinking the whole thing soon becomes peculiarly abstract and baffling. But if we are to under-

stand the particular nature of our present debate about God we
shall have to try to come to grips with certain broad features of
this question about knowledge.

There was once a Victorian head of a college in Oxford who
seemed, even in that age of giants, to be a particular embodiment
of authoritative and educated awareness. Of him it was written:

> I am the master of this college,
> and what I don't know isn't knowledge.

This, of course, was written with tongue in cheek, but it does
suggest the impression made by a man who has somehow won a
position of impressive authority and who occupies it in a way
which is generally judged to be competent. And what this not
very serious example draws attention to is the way in which what
we take for knowledge is connected with the people whom we
are prepared to listen to, that is to say, there is a very close
connection between whom we regard as 'authorities' and what
we regard as knowledge. I would suggest that today anyone
who counts as a scientist (whatever may be the precise
definition of this term) counts also, without having to establish
his claim, as an authority. We would not say of him that what he
does not know is not knowledge because we are aware that one
of the great things about Science is that it is always finding out
new things. But we might well say that what he *cannot* know is
not knowledge.

This, of course, is a gross over-simplification. I have not
defined 'science' or 'scientists' or even 'we'. But I am trying to
describe the general climate of opinion in which we operate and
which more or less affects all of us, consciously or unconsciously,
with regard to the matter of knowledge. It is necessary to do this
because there is the closest possible connection between what we
accept as knowledge and what we are prepared to think really
exists. What you can know is 'there' to be known, what you

cannot know is not 'there' at all, or perhaps we should say is
neither here nor there. If, therefore, our idea of knowledge is
deeply influenced or even determined by our understanding of
what a scientist as a scientist can or might find out, then we are
liable to take for granted that the only things which are
'there' are things with which the scientist as scientist can deal. In
fact, if you want to *know*, he is the man who can tell you. And if
what you want to know about is the sort of thing about which he
cannot tell you, then it becomes very doubtful whether that sort
of thing is a real sort of thing at all. Facts are facts and everything
else is a mere matter of belief, opinion, attitude, taste, where one
man's meat may be another man's poison, or, at any rate, everyone must be left to make his own subjective choice, for there is
no-one in a position to tell you with the sort of authority which
the scientist has, by reason of the practice of his science.

The relevance of all this to the debate about God is probably
already clear and indeed all this has doubtless occurred to you
long ago. But I fancy that the debate about God has exploded in
the way it has recently in this country because we have just got
round to the attempt to face the questions posed by the scientific
attitude in an open and general way, instead of leaving them to be
discussed only at an academic and sophisticated level. It is worth
while, therefore, to try and clarify the central question about
knowledge a little further.

In the world in which Christianity arose there was quite as
much debate about reality, the meaning of life, and the existence
and nature of God as there is today. The decisive difference for
our discussion lies in the type of man who was most likely to be
taken as authoritative, and in the type of data or understanding
which was most likely to be taken as knowledge. We have our
present type of debate about God because the situation then and
now is precisely reversed. Then the prevailing climate of opinion
took it for granted that the sort of things you straightforwardly

observed with your senses and which made up the ordinary stuff of life were mere appearances, and that the really real could only be grasped by those who were able to penetrate beyond and behind the veil of appearances to the true and unchanging reality which the appearance distorted or hid. The man in whom you might reasonably decide to put your trust as a source of knowledge, as one who could tell you what you wanted to know about the reality of yourself and the world, would be a philosopher or priest who either by the powers of his own mind or spirit, or because he had received a revelation, was in a position to lead you from the appearances to the reality. Observations of mere phenomena could not give you knowledge. That lay with the man who could lead you beyond such phenomena into the realm of mind and spirit freed from material things. But today the man whose authority to tell you things is taken for granted is precisely the man who has been trained in scientific methods of observing phenomena and who bases what he has to say on a corpus of knowledge built up by observation and experiment and constantly verified by further processes of practice and observation. Knowledge is closely connected with 'know-how'. You have knowledge if you can understand how processes work in such a way that you can reproduce them, put them right when they go wrong, and invent new uses for them. The man who can tell you with authority, i.e. so that you will take what he says from him although you yourself are not personally acquainted with the facts and reasons, is the man who is scientifically trained.

It is, I think, no use protesting that this is a hopelessly over-simplified picture in at least two respects, true as the protest would be. Firstly, it can be alleged that what I have been trying to say about the scientifically trained man is simply an uncritical acceptance of the myth of science. In reality, when a proper and sophisticated attention is given to the scientific method, the history of scientific development and the present state of the philosophy of science, it becomes clear that one does not have to conclude that the scientific approach itself leaves no room for the dimension of mystery in the universe. Secondly, it may be protested that the tradition which sets greater store by spiritual insight than by the results of observations of phenomena is by no means overwhelmed in the modern world. Such protests would certainly direct attention to areas which require investigation, but this investigation is part of the continuing debate. What I am trying to do is to describe the pressures which force the debate into the particular shape which it now takes. What it comes to is this.

When you consider the matter carefully, what each one of us knows in the direct sense of that with which we are directly and personally acquainted, is a very small part indeed of what we should be prepared to accept as knowledge. Most of what we accept as knowledge is that which comes to us 'on authority'. Consequently, what we count as knowledge is directly related to whom we are prepared to accept as authorities. Once upon a time the philosopher, the priest, the prophet, and perhaps the poet, were acceptably authoritative men. When you accepted them as authorities, you accepted what they said as knowledge, and when you accepted this as knowledge you accepted at the same time (indeed, it meant the same thing) that the things you were told about really existed or were the stuff of reality. Today, the type of man who is acceptably authoritative for nearly all the time by the vast majority of people is the scientist. Therefore the predominating picture of what is knowledge is determined by what he tells us, and this means that the things which are taken for granted as really existing and as providing the pattern for what is really real are the things about which he can tell us. Even if my sketch of the 'scientist' is simply an outline reflecting the 'myth' of science, nonetheless it is this 'myth' which decisively influences the view which most of us have about knowledge and reality.

The debate about God, therefore, must be carried on with a full awareness of the pressures of this 'myth'. Indeed, it is a debate about whether the myth is simply one more myth, the latest of a succession of purely human views of the world against which belief in God has always had to battle, or whether it is a view of the reality of things which more nearly corresponds to the way things really are than any previous view, so that theism as a possible view is being finally squeezed out.

The authority of the scientist within his own sphere is taken for granted. So much so that the type of authoritativeness which he has, and the data with which he deals, which is the subject matter and the basis of his knowledge, are taken as definitive of what authority is, and what is data and what is knowledge. As the scientific method is held to be based on the observation of data, formulation of hypotheses on the basis of observed data and verification of these hypotheses by further use of the experimental methods which were used to collect data in the first place, it is clear that scientific knowledge is confined to those types of things which can or might provide data for the experimental method. That is to say, scientific knowledge is necessarily confined to objects which can be observed in a scientific way. If scientific knowledge is the type of what may be taken as knowledge at all, then it follows that we can know only the sort of things which science can discover for us. But, as we have already seen, there is a close connection between that which can be known and that which is really 'there'. So if we can have knowledge only of the sort of things which can be discovered by scientific methods, then these are the only sort of things which really exist. Any other 'thing' is in reality only the product of the human imagination and however important to human life such 'things' may be, they do not really exist, and are no real part of the real world.

When the conclusion is put as bluntly and as crudely as this, very many people would want to deny it, or at least to say that they would wish to remain in a position of agnosticism in which they are not prepared either to deny or to affirm this materialistic position. But what we must be clear about in considering the debate about God is that it is, to the mind of most people today, manifest that science does put you meaningfully and practically in touch with things that are really there. The evidence for this is quite simply the fact that science enables you to do so many things and also that anyone who can get himself sufficiently trained in any branch of science will be able to communicate freely and successfully with anyone else who has the same training in the same science. Whatever difficulties subtle philosophers may be able to think up within the philosophy of science and about the problems of communication between persons, it is quite sufficiently clear to ordinary common sense that scientists are on to something which must be there, because of what they are able to do with the data they obtain. Thus, whether or not there are other 'things' to be known, it is certain for all practical purposes that there are scientific things to be known. So the scientist does not have to establish any claim to authority or any claim to be one who knows. He is authoritative because he does know.

Now God, according to the understanding of those who believe in Him, however much He may be related to and present in the universe, is held to be the Other who is also wholly different from the universe. At any rate, this is the view of God held hitherto within the biblical tradition, and this is the view which we are discussing when we are discussing the possibility of the end of theism. There can be absolutely no doubt, therefore, that the God of theism is not a 'thing' which is knowable within the terms of scientific knowledge. If, therefore, scientific knowledge is the pattern of knowledge, the God of the theists is not knowable. But that which is not knowable is not 'there', so if scientific knowledge is the pattern of knowledge the God of the theists does not exist.

It is really all a question of data. We know the sort of things which constitute scientific data, and we are not inclined to doubt that they exist. What could constitute data for non-scientific 'things'? The debate about God is really a confrontation between the undoubted givenness of that with which the scientist deals and—what? What I propose to do in the rest of the book is to draw attention to the ways in which certain influential theologians have reacted to this question. The theologians in question, Bultmann, Barth and Brunner, Tillich and Bonhoeffer have been selected because their thought has been so influential on the pace-making contributors from the Christian side to the present debate. This is not to be wondered at, because they have all been particularly open to, and conscious of, the pressures on belief in God, which are to be found in the modern scientific world view. I do not myself think that these theologians, all of whom are Protestants, can alone provide all that the Christian requires or all that the Christian tradition has to offer for living in the debate. I shall return to this point in my final chapter. But I do think that the theologians in question are of the utmost importance in facing up to the debate, because they have not been protected from the full rigours and erosions of the scientific world view by the institution and prestige of the Church in the manner of their colleagues of the Roman Communion. (I do not especially wish to accuse Roman Catholic theologians of escapism or obscurantism. I wish only to point out that it is the Protestant continental theologians who have so far been most acutely affected by the situation I am trying to outline.)

However, it is, I think, easier to understand currents of thought which are fully developed and in full (and bewildering!) flood if one goes a bit back into history and first takes a look at a point where the currents are recognizably beginning to eddy up and separate out into the streams which some people think are by now finally washing away the ground upon which believers in

God have taken their stand. If we have some understanding of the historical development of certain ideas we shall be in a much better position to estimate the force which they at present ought to have and we shall also be less inclined to panic if we discover that what we had supposed to be a suddenly arising and over-whelming new wave is in reality one more large-sized ripple on a stream which has been flowing for some time—and that the stream has not so far washed away as much as might be thought. (If I may take an already over-extended metaphor a little further I should like to add that I believe that we shall also find that the stream has significant life-giving qualities as far as the living religion of the living God is concerned, but this aspect must be left to be touched upon at the end of the book.)

I propose, therefore, to take up some discussions from the eighteenth century as a means of illuminating and pin-pointing our problems of the twentieth, and as a bridge to our considera-tion of the present day theologians I have mentioned. This will at least make clear that 'The End of Theism?' is not a new question and it will, I think, also make it clear that it has not even been raised in a new way. The beginnings of the way in which Bishop Robinson raised the question 'The End of Theism?' are to be found at least at the end of the eighteenth century. The develop-ments in human thought which gave rise to this way of raising the question lie, of course, much earlier—wherever 'modern scientific thinking' arose—but at the point which I have chosen we can see the debate taking on much of its current shape. To study this emergence should assist us to clarity of understanding and to study it at a stage which is removed from us by one hundred and fifty years or more should allow us to keep a little cooler than the pressures of current debate sometimes allow. And if we are to live effectively and creatively in and with a current debate which must exercise the very greatest pressures upon us, then clarity and coolness will be very necessary for us.

Chapter Two

SCIENCE, REASON AND FAITH
SOURCES OF DATA FOR OUR ATTITUDE TO THE WORLD

I PROPOSE TO carry on our investigation therefore by contrasting the approach used in commending the Christian faith by Bishop Butler in 1736, and by Friedrich Schleiermacher in 1799. This is not a piece of antiquarianism, because Bishop Butler represents a method of apology and argument which goes right back into the Christian tradition (and which I myself think must, in however changed a form, have its equivalent today), while Schleiermacher can reasonably be regarded as the innovator of a modern form of apologetics, and he certainly has had a great influence, whether by action or reaction, on the theologians we are to consider. That the introduction of Schleiermacher into a book on the current debate is justified will, I hope, become clear as we discover that a great deal of that which comes up in *Honest to God* or lies behind it is to be found, explicitly or implicitly, in Schleiermacher.

Bishop Butler dated the 'advertisement' to the first edition of his *Analogy of Religion* May 1736. In it he wrote: 'It is come, I know not how, to be taken for granted, by many persons, that Christianity is not so much as a subject of enquiry; but that it is, now at length, discovered to be fictitious. And accordingly they treated it as if in the present age this were an agreed point among all people of discernment; and nothing remained but to set it up as a principal subject of mirth and ridicule, as it were by way of reprisals, for its having so long interrupted the pleasures of the world.' He proposed, however, to show that there was a clear case for the truth of Christianity, as any reasonable man would have to admit. 'There is, I think, strong evidence of its truth; but it is certain no-one can upon principles of reason, be satisfied of the contrary.' What is of interest to us, beyond noting the fact that Christianity had been written off among 'people of discernment' well over two hundred years ago, is the shape which Bishop Butler gave to his book.

He divided it into two parts, the first entitled *Of Natural Religion* and the second entitled *Of Revealed Religion*. It is clear, even from a glance at the list of contents, that a good deal of use, at any rate in the first part, is made of arguments connected with morality. Bishop Butler is faced with educated men who take it for granted that there is no case for Christianity. Against them he appeals to the authorities of reason and of revelation and within the appeal to reason he includes an appeal to the moral sense. He is clearly a believer in what is called 'natural theology'. That is, he holds that it is possible by directing the attention of reasonable men to reasonable arguments relating to the nature of the world, the nature of men and the nature of men's life in the world, to show that something may be discovered and known about the existence of God and even to some extent about His nature. In terms of the discussion that we have set out above, he believes that it is reasonably possible to direct attention to the data which any fair-minded person studying science or reflecting on morality would agree *is* data and which point to the discovery of God. It is not until he has drawn attention to this type of data that he goes on to the data of revealed religion. This is the normal pattern of Christian apologetic, worked out in its most classical form in the Middle Ages by Thomas Aquinas.

Since, as I have already said, (p. 19), there is a sense in which the present debate about God may be seen as all a question of data, it is worthwhile to notice what this pattern of apologetic implies and assumes about data with regard to Christianity. It is, that there are two sources of data which can supply the actual content of Christian belief or, at least, lead to its acceptance. These are commonly and shortly described as Reason and Revelation. Reason is a source because proper (i.e. reasonable) attention to and thinking about the ordinary facts and patterns of the world which science studies, leads one on to the conclusion that the existence of these facts in these patterns requires the existence of a Source and Orderer of such facts and patterns (or makes it probable that such a Being exists or, at least, that it is reasonable to accept the existence of such a Being if there is what is alleged to be evidence from another source concerning such a Being). Reasonable attention to the natural world produces natural religion. This type of thinking has usually held that it has access to data which takes one some way beyond the mere existence of the Being who is the Author of beings. Certain facts about His character may reasonably be inferred, especially when consideration is given to the ethical and moral aspects of human life in the world (cf. the shape of the *Of Natural Religion* part of Bishop Butler's book already referred to). In view of the form which the argument we are to follow takes from Schleiermacher onwards, I would summarize the point about Reason as a source of data for religion by saying that this type of apologetic assumes that data to support or even to be built into the Christian Faith can be found from that which is the data of Science and that which is the data of Morality.

Then there is revelation as a distinct source of data. This type of data exists because God does not leave Himself to be discovered solely or even primarily by careful and reasonable attention to and reflection upon the data of science and of morality. He also takes the initiative in making Himself known. This activity of God has resulted in His being known and understood in a way which even the deepest insight into natural data would not open up to men. (It is important to note that at its heart this tradition of revelation has never claimed that through it has come complete data about God or full knowledge of God. God remains a mystery far beyond the facts about Him made known through the data of revelation.) This revealed data came through God's action to particular men and through particular events, and the data so received and perceived is set down in the Bible. Hence the Bible is the effective, practical source of revealed data. To put it crudely, the position is that from the world you can read off the existence of God and from the Bible you can read off the character of God. This is very crude and over-simplified but it does, I think, show sufficiently the essential structure of the traditional position with regard to the sources of data about God.

Why are 'people of discernment' mistaken in supposing that Christianity is 'discovered to be fictitious'? Because Reason operating on the world with which Science and Morality are concerned sufficiently indicates the outlines of that Divine Being the details of whose character of love and work of salvation are filled in for us by the Revelation recorded in the Bible. Reason prepares the ground for Revelation while Revelation surpasses Reason in a manner which Reason herself on reflection can see in fact fulfils her understandings and aspirations. Modern believers may already wish to throw away this book with the protest that this sort of thing does not touch the heart of Christian believing at all. As we shall shortly see (if the book is not thrown away!) Schleiermacher would entirely agree with them. Modern un-believers may well feel that this *exposé* of the traditional basis for commending Christianity shows quite clearly why 'we are all atheists now' (including the modern believers!). I, however, am contending that unless we unravel the actual historical development of the arguments a little we probably shall not be able to avoid being prematurely confused by popular and frequent allegations about what is, nowadays, 'thinkable'. We should, surely, give some attention to what people actually did think and to the reasons why they thought what they did. Then we should consider what we think and why. And after that we ought to give some consideration to the question whether it is only what 'they' found thinkable which needs revising. There would seem to be some danger in taking it for granted that a current climate of thought (what an alleged or even actual majority of 'us' find thinkable) is wholly determinative of what is true. At least, if this is our assumption, we ought to be clear that it is and that we find this assumption satisfactory. And to this end we shall surely find helpful a study of the way a line of thought developed and a consideration of it in relation to that which such thinking was reacting against. We start, therefore, with Butler, who found the basis of the truth of the Christian religion in a combination of revelation and reason. Reason did its work by considering tha which was the data of science and of morality. Revelation was drawn from the data provided primarily by the Bible.

When Schleiermacher comes in 1799 to publish his work *On Religion—Speeches to Its Cultured Despisers*, he does not use this pattern at all. In his second speech he writes that religion 'resigns at once all claim on anything that belongs either to science or morality'. In making this move he is taking full account of the views of the cultured despisers of religion, for he says to them, 'You would never grant that our faith is as surely founded or stands on the same level of certainty as your scientific knowledge'. This is *the* point which is our point as much as Schleiermacher's. 'Our faith', 'your scientific knowledge' and 'the same level of certainty'. 'Faith' and 'scientific knowledge' are to be firmly put apart because of difficulties over 'levels of certainty'. And these are closely connected with the contrasting means by which the data of scientific knowledge and the deliverances of faith are obtained. This is the nub of our problem As I have already said, 'the debate about God is really a confrontation between the undoubted givenness of that in which the scientist deals and—what?' Schleiermacher does not believe that you can reasonably go on from the givenness of this scientific data to see that there is room, basis and need for religious faith. Faith ('our faith') and scientific knowledge ('your scientific knowledge') *are* on different 'levels' with regard to the way in which we are certain or assured of that which they have to do. But, none the less, the deliverances of faith are the source from which the data to be set alongside the data of science is to be obtained. If this diagnosis of the situation is correct, then the question at issue about God may well be seen as whether this former data (the data of faith) is real data at all. That is to say, can it at all 'count' against or in relation to the data of science and if so what does it count for and how does it count? The whole of the book is really about these questions so we shall constantly be returning to them, but for the time being I think it will be helpful to point up the contrast between Butler and Schleiermacher.

Butler finds *continuity* between our knowledge of the world, our understanding of morality and our apprehension of religion (although we need revelation to take religion far enough). Schleiermacher admits, indeed insists on, *discontinuity*. For Butler that which 'belongs either to science or morality' is not sufficient for the revealed theism which is the Christian religion, but is part of the whole understanding of things and of the knowledge of true reality which is covered by and contained in Christianity and which can certainly lead up to the acceptance of Christianity or at least gain a hearing for Christianity which may lead to its acceptance. For Schleiermacher, that on which religion is based has nothing directly to do with that which gives rise to science and morality. Certainly religion in no way depends upon the processes of knowing involved in science nor on those of discernment involved in morality. It is a serious mistake, he holds, as well as a hopeless undertaking to try and gain a hearing for Christianity by appealing either to our ordinary and scientific knowledge of the world or to our understanding of morality.

Put in terms of the question about data, Schleiermacher sees the position as follows. There is one type of data which is produced by and forms the subject matter of the human activity of knowing. Knowing is a distinct human activity which is to do with consciousness of the external world developed and articulated by men as they perceive all the things which are or can be objects for them. The objects of knowledge are a distinct type of data (just as knowing is a distinct human activity) and they form the subject matter of Science. Besides *knowing*, which is a passive human 'activity' and remains within the knower, there is also *doing*, which is a practical outgoing activity directed to producing effects on or in relation to objects which are or might be known. Just as science covers the sphere of knowing, so morality covers the sphere of doing. As we have just seen, according to Schleiermacher religion resigns all claims on anything that belongs to either of these spheres. Science is the sum-total of the data arrived at by a proper exercise of the human capacity for knowing. Morality is the sum-total of the data arrived at by a proper reflection on the human experience of doing. In knowing and in doing men do not get on to data which if 'looked at in the proper way' will become data for or part of the data of religion. That is to say that you cannot take a selection of the data of science or morality and show that this selection reasonably raises questions which point to religious answers, answers which when given and accepted show that this data, besides being the data of science or morality, is also data for religion.

I think that an example (my own and not his) of what Schleiermacher's approach means is that you cannot pass from a scientific insight into the way certain things are patterned in the physical universe directly, and by the same activity of the human mind which perceives such a pattern, into a religious insight that the world is created, or into a perception of the Creator. It is in this sense that religion 'resigns ... all claims on anything that belongs either to science or to morality'. Religion is no longer to imagine that she can establish her claim to be heard as having something meaningful, true and important to say by appealing to such data. The data of science and the data of morality are the data of science and the data of morality, and that is that. Religion must look elsewhere for all or any of her subject-matter and basis and there must be some human 'activity' other than those of knowing and doing which is the source, from the human end, of religion. This is what I meant by saying that Schleiermacher insists on discontinuity in these spheres.

He does not think for one moment that he is surrendering to science by accepting and developing this separation. On the contrary he believes that he is simply bringing to the front what has always been the true nature of religion. 'Belief', he maintains, 'must be something different from a mixture of opinion about God and the world and of precepts for one life or for two. Piety cannot be an instinct for a mess of ethical and metaphysical crumbs'. (p. 31). ('Piety', as we shall shortly see, is Schleiermacher's significant word for religion.) The arid Christian expositors and apologists of the period between the dying down of the fervent fires of the Reformation and the end of the eighteenth century when Schleiermacher was writing had reduced the Christian religion to a way of looking at the world ('metaphysical crumbs') and to the provision of what was supposed to be a divinely undergirded set of rules for the conduct of life which had the sanction of future heavenly punishment and reward ('ethical crumbs' and 'precepts for one life or two'). Such a reduction of the living and personal Christian Faith in effect both kills true religion and ensures that religion is despised by cultured men who, by definition, are competently aware of what is going on in science, metaphysics and morals. Therefore, reasons Schleiermacher, to restore religion to its living reality and to restore to it its own authentic authority and claim to be heard, it is necessary drastically and definitively to disentangle it from science and morality.

But it is very important to notice here that there are two points involved which are not necessarily connected. It is one thing to be clear that religion (and above all the Christian religion) is something different from, or at least more than, a combination of views about the world and precepts for morality. It is quite another to decide that religion 'resigns . . . all claims on anything that belongs to science and morality'. To insist, as is surely right, that a living religious faith has its heart, basis and goal in something other than some metaphysics and some morality it is not necessary to surrender to the notion that the data and proper subject-matter of science, morality and religion must be kept carefully and as a matter of essential theory separated from one another.

If you insist on this type of complete separation between knowledge regarded primarily and definitively as that which science gives you, morality, and religion, the probability surely is that you will soon reach the following position. What is scientifically known will be taken for granted as real. It is 'hard' data. It will also be possible to hold that there is some sort of reality in whatever it is that morality deals with. Certainly in choosing, caring, righting wrongs and so on we are 'up against' something or other. Although precisely what we are up against, and in precisely what sense we are up against it, will not be so easy to determine as in the case of science. But when we then proceed to what we have decided is the totally distinct and separate sphere of religion, we shall be very hard put to it to find anything at all which we can be up against. We shall probably conclude that the data lies in science and in some sort of way in morality, but that religion has no data. In which case religion can surely be dispensed with for it is not 'about anything'.

This is precisely what has happened in our current debate. We are said to be at the end of theism. We are recommended to turn to 'religionless' or 'secular' Christianity as the only version of Christianity which can be entertained (i.e. is 'thinkable') today. We are to find the reality with which religion has hitherto been concerned in an attitude and policy towards the realities of the universe as known to science and the realities experienced in our dealings with and relations between persons. These exhaust the possibilities of reality that there are and we are told that it is no longer possible to conceive of, still less to have dealings with, reality which is totally different from and transcendent of these realities. God is out though godly attitudes may be in.

In view of the very strong appeal which this whole line of argument clearly has at the present time, it is necessary to under-stand something of its origins if we are to come to any reasonable conclusion as to whether this reduction of religious reality to an adverb which some people choose to use in characterizing substantive reality (i.e. that reality that is really there!) is possible or necessary. Hence the excursion in which we are engaged into the history of the climate of opinion with regard to the claims which can or ought to be made for paying heed to religion. And I am simply pointing out at the moment that the move which Schleiermacher made when, under the pressure of the growing prestige of science, he gladly agreed to separate out science, morality, and religion in a radical way, is a very dangerous one for religion. Of course, it may be an inevitable one, but in that case my own judgment would be that religion in any sense which is continuous with that of the beliefs and attitudes central to the Bible would indeed be finished. But here we are back to what the debate is about and we are concerned at the moment with ob-taining guidance in it, so we must be content with trying to understand both the reasons which led to the making of this move for separateness and the dangers which lie in it.

Schleiermacher, as you will already have gathered, was convinced that, far from putting the religion of the Bible in danger,
he was liberating and establishing it. For he was sure that, beside
and distinct from knowing and doing, there was another activity
of the human spirit and that it was in and through this third
activity that religion found, from the human end, its proper,
distinct and assured basis. This was the activity of *feeling*. Naturally
he was referring to 'feeling' in a particular sense of the term. He
did not mean mere feeling or any feelings you like but 'immediate self-consciousness'. He added the description 'immediate'
to distinguish the essential type of feeling he was concerned with
from that sort of self-consciousness in which we are aware of
ourselves as objects to ourselves. Examples of this objective type
of self-consciousness which is *not* feeling would be when we are
conscious of ourselves as being angry and we therefore reproach
ourselves, or when we observe ourselves keeping our angry
feelings in check and so approve of ourselves. Here self-consciousness is to do with knowing and judging and so comes into those
spheres of knowing and doing which we have already considered
and from which feeling is to be distinguished. *Immediate* self-
consciousness is not the accompaniment of a state but the direct
experience of the state itself. Examples which Schleiermacher
gives are joy and sorrow. These may follow from self-approval
and self-reproach but there is no element of knowing or judging
about them. They just are—feelings. Feeling in this sense is a
direct, immediate and independent activity of the human spirit.
Knowing is a form of human consciousness or activity which
rests within the knower but is concerned with objects external to
him. Doing is a human consciousness or activity which passes
outside the doer and, of course, has reference to objects external
to him. But feeling is *wholly inward*. This is of the utmost importance and a significant clue to be borne in mind with regard
to the whole debate about God. For note that Schleiermacher

is locating the basis of religion in *pure subjectivity*. If this is the sole and proper basis for religion how long will it be possible or proper to maintain that religion is anything more than an attitude (God will be out although godly attitudes may remain in —see p. 30 above)? However, this is what he is doing and that deliberately and with satisfaction. He does not believe that he is putting God 'out' (the beginning of the end of theism?) but that he is showing precisely where and how God is 'in'.

Religion, in Schleiermacher's judgment, is best referred to and described by the term 'piety' which describes the characteristic attitude of the religious man to life and the world at large. Now the essence of piety is the consciousness (i.e. feeling—see above) of being absolutely dependent. An imaginative effort must be made to appreciate the inwardness of what Schleiermacher is seeking to describe here, and that for at least three inter-connected reasons. Firstly, he is directing attention to what, I am sure, is an essential element in any knowledge of God which can truly claim to be 'knowledgelike' i.e., in terms of our previous discussion, a real source of real data. Secondly, this 'feeling of absolute dependence' is, as Tillich himself says, 'rather near to what is called... "ultimate concern about the ground and meaning of our being".' (Tillich, *Systematic Theology* I p. 47.) So if we are to understand these notions of 'ultimate concern' and 'ground of being' which have loomed so large in the current debate we must appreciate something of Schleiermacher's meaning and intention. Thirdly, and this is really only a particular reflection of the first point, this feeling or consciousness is direct and therefore self-authenticating. Hence in seeking to describe it Schleiermacher is making his contribution to answering the most difficult and most central question of the whole debate about God viz: What do you mean by 'God'? Where do you get the experiential and experimental material which forms the basis, or is the nucleus, of your idea of God, your meaning for the word 'God', your 'placing' of God in relation to your overall understanding of and approach to the universe as a whole? His answer is that your feeling of absolute dependence is that basis and that it is the only basis, the only possible basis. I shall argue later that, in fixing on this 'feeling of absolute dependence' as not only necessary to any real knowledge of God but also as its sufficient and only possible basis, Schleiermacher was making an understandable but potentially disastrous mistake which is still very much alive and productive of effects in the current debate. Indeed I am sure that it is absolutely central to the current debate. Hence this present extended discussion to show the pressures and attitudes which lead *to* the mistake. In the rest of the book we shall have to consider the effects *of* the mistake and, indeed, why it *is* a mistake. Now we must try and understand what Schleiermacher is getting at in fixing on this 'feeling of absolute dependence' and we can do so by developing the interdependence of the three points which I have just made.

First, then, the point about the 'feeling of absolute dependence' as an essential element in any knowledge of God. If God exists and if He is God, then the only 'thing' which in the long run can *establish* that God exists is God Himself. How do we establish that any 'thing' is 'there' i.e. really exists? We are back to the question of data—that which is given to us. If we get a sufficient number of 'impressions' of a 'thing', other people get them too, and we find that by one means or another we and other people can bring it about that these 'impressions' are repeated, then we take it for granted that the 'thing' is indeed 'there'. We therefore treat it as part of the 'data' of our experience and material to be built into our knowledge. But the 'impressions' which 'things' produce, the data which we obtain, are clearly sufficient to establish the existence (the 'really being there') only of the sorts of 'things' which furnish or are the data in the first place. That is to say that 'thing-like' impressions can only impress you with the existence

of 'thing-like' things. Things provide data that establish the
existence of themselves or other things.

Now it may or may not be the case that reasonable reflection on
'the way things are' produces some sort of impression that in some
sense or other there 'is' 'More than' just thing-like things. And it
may or may not be the case that it is possible to receive or
apprehend 'impressions' of the 'More than' as such. But the
'impression' in either of these cases would be decisively different
in kind from the impressions which are, or which provide, the
data for establishing the existence of things. This 'impression' of
the 'existence' of the 'More than' must be so very different from
'data-impressions' for two reasons. First because of its source and
second because of its 'object'. As to its source, *this* 'impression' is
not produced by some one thing or by any particular group of
things simply as things. For such impressions of 'things in
particular' simply serve to establish the existence of particular
things. *This* is an impression made by 'the way things are' or
'things as a whole', 'things in general'. Hence it is an impression of
a very different kind from those impressions which are normally
associated with what is normally considered to be 'data'. Secondly
as to 'object', if the 'More than' of which there is supposed to be
this special type of impression is truly more than the sum total of
existing particular things, then any 'impression' which such a
'More than' produces must be an impression of a type peculiar
to 'it' and which 'it' alone can produce. Things produce thing-
like impressions and thing-like impressions can establish only the
existence of things. But the 'More than' is, by definition, not a
thing (being 'more than' things) and so cannot produce a thing-
like impression. Conversely the 'More than' alone would be
sufficient to produce the impression which established that 'it'
'existed'. It might be the case that impressions of things or an
impression produced by impressions of things raised a question
whether there was 'Something' more than things. But if you have

a question as to *whether* something exists you have to look for data to *establish* its existence. Ordinary data establishes ordinary existence. If the existence of this extraordinary 'Something' or 'More than' is to be established, there must be extraordinary data. But the only data which would be extraordinary enough for the task would be data as extraordinary as the 'More than' 'itself' and this, presumably, could only *be* the 'More than' 'itself'. Now the God of theism has always been understood to be 'transcendent' i.e. passing over or being more than all existent things. Hence the statement two paragraphs ago which began this particular part of the argument that if God exists and if he is God then the only 'thing' which in the long run can *establish* that God exists is God Himself.

The liberal and, I fear, clumsy-seeming use of inverted commas in the foregoing may perhaps be excused if it can be seen that this use serves to pinpoint why, in the present debate about God, the question of the end of theism is raised. 'Impression' goes into inverted commas because an impression produced or alleged to be produced by things in general may very well be held to be something quite different from those impressions of particular things which are ordinarily recognized as providing data for our knowledge of the world and the ways of things in the world. An overall impression of this nature may seem much more like an opinion or attitude which some people may have than a piece of knowledge or a basis of information which everyone must have. Secondly, 'it', 'itself', 'object' and 'thing' go into inverted commas because the point about mentioning the 'More than' at all is precisely that 'it' is not thing-like but goes beyond and is radically different from all existing things. That is to say that the 'More than' is not an object or thing in any ordinary sense of those words and consequently 'it' should not be referred to as 'it' or 'itself' in any ordinary sense of *those* words. But this leads on to the reason for putting 'is' and 'existed' in inverted commas. As I have just said above 'ordinary data establishes ordinary existence'. If the 'More than' is not object-like or thing-like then there is no question of ordinary data establishing ordinary existence. So 'is' and 'existed' when used of the 'More than' are not used in the ordinary senses of those words. Or at least—and this is really the crux of the whole matter—it might seem very likely that if your 'data' has to go into inverted commas (because it is extraordinary and not ordinary) then the sense in which such 'data' 'establishes' 'something' as 'existing' ought to go into inverted commas too. But since what the inverted commas stand for is 'not in the ordinary sense' we might well find ourselves coming to the conclusion that the correct way to translate all this is to say that the 'More than' cannot be established (in the ordinary sense) as existing (in the ordinary sense). And what is the difference between that and saying that God does not, in the ordinary sense of the word, exist? If there is an overall impression connected with things in general which demands to be reckoned with then we may be required or at least recommended to adopt a particular attitude which takes account of this without getting involved in any talk of some 'More than' *existing*. We are once again back to the conclusion that God is out although godly attitudes may remain in.

This time we have seen the possibility of this conclusion coming up by considering the question 'How do we establish that any "thing" is "there" i.e. really exists?' Previously we encountered this possibility (realized in the current debates) when we were considering the sharp separation of the spheres of science and morality from that of religion. It is of the highest importance to notice that we have come up against this possibility of deciding that a godly attitude might have to be substituted for belief in God from two very different ends. One could be described as the apologetic, the other as the ontological. An apologetic approach is determined by asking and answering the question 'How shall we persuade people to think the thoughts that we think they

ought to think?' That is to say that anything apologetic necessarily takes its tone from the way people do as a matter of fact
think (their current habits or thought). An ontological approach,
in so far as it is a distinctive possibility, is (or would be) determined in the end not by the prevalent habits of thinking but by
the reality of that which one is attempting to think about. (The
word 'ontological' is based on a part of the Greek verb 'to be'
and refers, therefore, to that which is rooted in or concerned with
the 'be-ing' of things.)

Schleiermacher's sharp separation of religion from science and
morality arises from an apologetic concern. As I have already
quoted (p. 25 above), in his *On Religion—Speeches to Its Cultured
Despisers* he says to these despisers 'you would never grant that
our faith . . . stands on the same level of certainty as your scientific knowledge'. His approach to the whole question of the
knowledge of God is decisively affected (even if not largely
determined) by his judgment of what the 'cultured despisers' of
religion would grant. Since they would not grant any grounds
for religion as Schleiermacher understands it in Science or
Morality, religion 'resigns at once all claims on anything that
belongs either to science or morality'. So religion must base its
claim on 'immediate self-consciousness' with the attendant danger
to which I have drawn attention of turning out to be a purely
subjective attitude to things. But before going on to try to make
clear what Schleiermacher himself thought he was getting at
through this immediate self-consciousness, I pointed out that
whatever he precisely meant he was certainly on to something of
the utmost importance with regard to knowledge of God. This
was so, I have just argued (p. 33 above) because 'if God exists
and if He is God then the only 'thing' which in the long run
can establish that God exists is God Himself'. I have sought to
explain and justify *this* statement by trying to unpack what would
be the case about the existence of God if God existed. Thus we

have found ourselves attempting to approach the matter from the 'ontological' end. I have tried for a couple of paragraphs to set out what would be involved if a Being who could properly be called God could properly be said to exist. In doing this, however, we have come up against a strong case for such a liberal use of inverted commas around so many important words including the very word 'exist' that we have seen that there are grounds for doubting whether God can properly be said to exist. So whether you start from the way people do feel obliged to think or from the way it would seem one is obliged to think about God (if He is there to be thought about at all) one arrives at the same difficulty which is the point where the present debate about God is in fact focussed.

But this is precisely the point where Schleiermacher's potentially dangerous insistence on pivotting everything with regard to knowledge of God on immediate self-consciousness does draw attention to an essential element in the knowledge of God which has always been present within the Biblical and Christian understanding of Theism. It is this—that *the authenticating knowledge of God is not derived but direct.* By 'authenticating knowledge' I mean that knowing which, in the very experiencing of the knower, carries in that experience the assurance that it is indeed knowledge. Authenticating knowledge is knowledge which provides its own guarantee that it is truly knowledge i.e. that that which is thought to be being known is truly 'there' and is truly being known. Hence it is not 'derived' but 'direct'. One does not infer, or suppose, or even believe, that God exists (however proper or possible these operations may be in their place). God is known to one as existing. (I do *not* say that God is known *in His* existence because, according to this tradition, the totality of what is truly involved in God's being God is quite beyond human knowing. Direct knowledge of God in no way implies total knowledge of God.) This is simply to bring out the implications of the fact that the Biblical and Christian tradition of theism has always understood itself as having its ultimate basis both as a matter of fact and as a necessary matter of theory in *revelation*. The 'godness' of God makes it absolutely inevitable that the only way of being sure (i.e. having knowledge) that God exists lies in God's revealing himself (i.e. in God's making it possible for men to 'come up against him' directly). This notion has difficulties of its own but I am not at present concerned to discuss those. I wish simply to direct attention to this essential element in the tradition.

Revelation

The essential element is that there is involved in the establishment of knowledge of God a certain directness or underivedness of experience which has its own independent authenticity and authenticating weight. (In the tradition this is pointed out by referring to the necessity of God's revealing himself. Only God himself can establish that God exists. This is not the way Schleiermacher habitually talks but we shall look at that when we consider the effect of his apologetic approach.) In terms of the immediately preceding discussion of how one establishes something as being there (as really existing) this means that God is established as being there in a manner necessarily different from the manner in which everything else is established as existing. As the manner of establishing the fact of existence is different it is reasonable from one point of view to put all the words like 'thing', 'object' and 'existence' into inverted commas when talking about God. But as God *does* establish his existence to men (so the tradition of revelation affirms) it is necessary to recognize that the inverted commas are signs of warning that we are talking about God, and once that warning has been heeded they can perfectly well be removed (i.e. 'God exists' means what it says and 'exists' needs no special inverted commas of its own). They have to come back again whenever the warning is unheeded and men have fallen into the habit of talking and thinking about God as if he were on a par with all other existences and existents. But, if God is God (and only God can establish that!), there is no case for the permanent use of inverted commas. It follows from what is necessarily (although not completely) involved in God's being God that the use of inverted commas will always be a possibility and sometimes a necessity. But it follows from the fact that God is God that the basic way of talking about God must leave the inverted commas out. In talking, thinking and debating about God one cannot avoid the ontological question (the question of being) however much the tone of the debate is determined by the apologetic question (the question of current habits of thought) because if God is God (i.e. if God exists) we are confronted with unique existence, unique being, with reality which necessarily raises the question of what really is real. Or to put the matter the other way round—If one assumes that the answer to the apologetic question (how men habitually think) determines the answer to the ontological question (what there is to think about) one may well have already assumed that God does not exist. For God to be God must exist in a way which men do not necessarily think about—unless they are in the habit of having their ways of thinking conditioned by revelation in which God makes himself known.

But, and this is where one gets back to Schleiermacher, where does one get the evidence of this direct and authenticating experience of God in which God establishes himself? The apologetic climate certainly makes sure that we cannot get away from the question of evidence, of data. As I have already had occasion to remark twice, 'the debate about God is really a confrontation between the undoubted givenness of that in which the scientist deals and—what?' Schleiermacher is of such importance because he took the questions which the scientific approach poses to the Christian religion wholly seriously. Whatever errors lay in his method of doing this he was surely attempting what anyone who wishes to stand in the biblical and Christian tradition of theism must do. The doctrine of Creation demands that any approach which takes absolutely seriously the givenness (the data) of the Universe must itself be taken absolutely seriously (which does not necessarily mean taking it entirely on its own terms). For according to the Biblical understanding of things the data of the Universe is, in a real sense, God-given. Therefore the experimental approach is as much a necessary part of the Christian understanding of the Universe as it is of the Christian understanding of knowledge of God. When the experimental approach to the Universe puts in question the whole Christian claim to knowledge of God, then Christians are bound, by the logic of that knowledge of God which they claim to have, to see within that questioning a question posed by God himself. So the way to maintaining a living knowledge of God which has in it the essential element of self-authenticating directness is to face the questions with directness and openness in order that the question which God is posing is encountered, i.e. so that God is looked for to establish himself. When, therefore, the whole weight of the scientific approach raises the question of data, it is the question of data which must be faced. And this is the question which Schleiermacher does face.

On behalf of religion (which he is not seeking to establish but pass on. He speaks as a believer.) Schleiermacher appeals to the experienced and experimental data of feeling over against the data of knowing and doing (science and morality). I am arguing that in analysing out feeling (in the special sense of immediate self-consciousness) for separated emphasis with regard to the claims of religion to be true and meaningful, he was at least partially guided by a true instinct for an essential element in the Christian tradition of theism. He may have been moved to this emphasis chiefly by apologetic considerations but it contained ontological insight. For if you are to commend religion which is

Christian to cultured despisers in a modern tradition the real question to which you have to address yourself is not so much 'How do you know there is a God?' but rather 'What do you know when you are knowing God?' or 'What is it to know God?' Schleiermacher was surely right in being clear that the God with whom Christianity is concerned is not to be equated with that which rounds off a scientific view of the Universe or that which provides a basis for our moral understanding. There is nothing godlike about such a derived object. Of the true God there must be some direct awareness which serves somehow to put us on to that unique dimension which is the truly unique dimension of the existence of the truly unique God. But if God is not adequately conceived of as rounding off science or propping up morality and if, also, many men have lost the habit of entertaining the concept of God at all, then a self-conscious attempt must be made to point to that area of human experiencing in which such direct awareness is or may be found. And this attempt will be one necessary element at least in facing the question about data.

If we revert to the terms of the discussion of how we establish that something is 'there' (i.e. really exists) then the question about data with regard to God becomes something like 'How do we get an impression which is not object-like and which convincingly presents us with the reality of that which is 'More-than' the particular realities of the Universe?' Schleiermacher's answer to that is *in pious feeling* or *in immediate self-conscious-ness*. 'Piety' is his key-term for essential and true religion. It reflects his emphasis on the central importance of the inward experience of the believer. *Sole* emphasis on this, as I have already hinted and as I shall subsequently argue, is a mistake. *Some* emphasis on this, I am sure, essential. Let us now try and get clear what this pious feeling is and how it is alleged to work.

The essence of piety is the feeling of being absolutely dependent. This feeling of absolute dependence is the 'impression' we are

looking for which presents us with the self-authenticating awareness of God. It is not the result of, or derived from, any combination of the particular impressions produced by particular things.
It is the peculiar and unique impression which is produced by the
operation of 'the Whole' (as Schleiermacher puts it) upon us.
'What we feel and are conscious of in religious emotion is not the
nature of things, but their operation upon us' (*Speeches*; p. 48).
The nature of things is what Science investigates and we thereby
obtain knowledge of numerous series of detailed data and the
details of their inter-relations. But there is also the impression
which the whole of things makes upon us when we are open to
this in a particular form of attention. 'Religion is essentially
contemplative. You would never call anyone pious who went
about in impervious stupidity, whose sense is not open to the life
of the world. But this contemplation is not turned, as your
knowledge of nature is, to the existence of a finite thing, combined with and opposed to another finite thing' (i.e. to detailed
data in their inter-relations). . . The contemplation of the pious
is the immediate consciousness of the universal existence of all
finite things, in and through the Infinite, and of all temporal
things in and through the Eternal. Religion is to seek this and to
find it in all that lives and moves, in all growth and change, in all
doing and suffering. It is to have life and to know life in immediate feeling, only as such an existence in the Infinite and Eternal.
. . . It is a life in the infinite nature of the Whole, in the One and
in the All, in God, having and possessing all things in God, and
God in all. Yet religion is not knowledge and science, either of the
world or of God. Without being knowledge it recognizes knowledge and science. In itself it is an affection, a revelation of the
Infinite in the finite, God being seen in it and it in God' (*ib.* p. 36).

Religion draws its claims, indeed its strength and its assurance,
from an 'immediate consciousness', an 'immediate feeling', an
'affection' which is its own and peculiar to it. This arises, not as a

man strives to gain knowledge or to regulate his morality, but 'piety appears as a surrender, a submission to be moved by the Whole that stands over against man' (*ib.* p. 37). This 'Whole that stands over against man' (cf. Tillich's 'ultimate ground of our being') is experienced in and as the feeling of absolute dependence. In order to point out what he means by this, Schleiermacher draws attention to the fact that in regard to all that which makes up the universe a man feels relatively free and relatively dependent. This is to say that if you consider your relationship to any 'thing' you like in the world you will find that it involves a certain dependence. The thing obliges you to take its own particular form of 'thingness' seriously and to the extent to which it does that you are dependent upon it in your relationship with, and reaction to, it. But you are not absolutely dependent upon it. You have also your own relative freedom with regard to it. In so far as you have that you can, so to speak, impose your own terms on your relationship with this particular thing (within the limits of your dependence upon its being what it is). Thus a man's ordinary relationship to the ordinary things of the Universe involves awareness of relative freedom and relative dependence. (Recall, here, our earlier discussion about ordinary impressions establishing the existence of ordinary things.) But then Schleiermacher would have us turn our attention on this matter of freedom and dependence away from any particular impression of freedom or dependence in relation to any particular objects. He wants us to perceive and attend to a feature of self-consciousness which accompanies and underlies every particular awareness and is therefore a feature of self-consciousness as such. 'The self-consciousness which accompanies all our activity ... is itself precisely a consciousness of absolute dependence; for it is the consciousness that the whole of our spontaneous activity comes from a source outside of us ...' (*The Christian Faith* IV, 3). Ordinary awareness of our freedom and the way in which it is limited by a relative dependence upon the ordinary objects of the Universe has underlying it an awareness in what *we* might call the depth of the self-consciousness. (Schleiermacher himself does not talk about 'depth' but it is clear that one of the roots of the usage of 'depth'-language in the current debate does lie in his way of thinking. Freudian psychology is not the only source. And in any case Freud himself is not unaffected by currents of Romantic and Idealistic thinking which were already running in Schleiermacher's time.) This underlying awareness is an immediate feeling of absolute dependence upon 'the Whole that stands over against man'. If you do not recognize at all what this last discussion is about then piety has not so far been 'kindled' in you.

But it *can* be kindled in you, whoever you are and whatever at present you find 'thinkable', because this immediate consciousness of absolute dependence is a universal feature of human self-consciousness. It is at least latent in every human being insofar as he or she is a human being. It is universal at any rate as a potentiality because it just is the heart of what is involved in being a human being, and because it just is at the heart of what is involved in the relationship of each individual to the Universe as a whole. Of course, this is not a *proved* starting point for an approach to religion and to the question of God. It is a presupposed starting point. But it is not necessarily the worse for that. All starting points on matters of ultimate concern (if such there be—does it *really* matter to me that I am me?) are presuppositions and not proved propositions. And it would certainly seem at least highly probably true that if there is God then we can hope to be aware of Him only if there is, as part of our make-up, something which is already, in some sense, an awareness of Him. And once this awareness is kindled, once, that is, we begin to be 'truly pious', then we are directly aware that we are aware of God. This is an awareness which is quite independent of the knowings of Science or the doings of Morality, although Schleiermacher believes that

it reflects back on the whole of our lives and in some very powerful and decisively valuable way transfuses and transforms them.
(cf. passage from p. 36 of the *Speeches, cit. supra*.)

Now, for our purposes there is no need to become clearer about
just what it is that Schleiermacher is talking about in the type of
discussion which I have been trying to outline. Indeed, unless
you are the sort of person who vibrates significantly and excitedly
to the utterances of the Romantics you are very unlikely to *be*
clear just what it is that is being described. A further attempt at
understanding the content of Schleiermacher's thought would
require a much deeper investigation into his place in the history
of European thought since the middle of the eighteenth century.
What is important for our investigation into the present debate
about God is the form of Schleiermacher's argumentation and
exposition. Its shape is something like this. Attending to the
subject matter of Science and the subject matter of Morals will
not even get you looking in the direction of God or beginning
to feel a godly awareness (i.e.—?—in modern terms, enable you
to find the notion of God thinkable). Ordinary experience and
ordinary reflection on ordinary experience does not put you on
to God. But religion in general and Christianity in particular is
certainly about something. How, then, are we put on to, or how
do we become aware of, this 'something'? The answer is—in
religious experience, which is this unique feeling of absolute
dependence which is the same thing as consciousness of God. As
distinct from the 'givenness' of Science and Morality (their data)
we have God given in immediate self-consciousness, in and as the
feeling of absolute dependence.

The assumption of this whole line of approach is that such
God-consciousness or 'feeling for God' is, as a matter of fact, a
universal feature of any consciousness that can properly be called
human—all that is required is that a man will attend contempla-
tively to his own experiencing of the world so that he may become

aware, in a direct and immediate feeling, of that which underlies all his experience. Further, it is assumed that this feeling or awareness has built into it or, perhaps, is the same thing as, an all-embracing awareness of value, unity and fulfilment. (cf. the passage from p. 36 of the *Speeches* quoted at p. 43 above). It is this two-fold assumption which allows Schleiermacher to associate, indeed identify, this immediate self-consciousness with or substitute it for, knowledge of God and which also allows Tillich to make his characteristic use of the notions of ground of being and ultimate concern. For the first part of the assumption is that underlying all experience as such there is this feeling of absolute dependence. Now traditionally 'in the last analysis' that which 'underlies' everything (the First Cause, the Prime Mover, etc.) is God. So an immediate awareness which underlies all experience is an awareness of God. This identification is strengthened by the second part of the assumption. This is that the awareness has the value-effect of unifying and fulfilling. But once again, traditionally it is God who is the supreme Value, the unifying and fulfilling Good. Hence this worshipful-like awareness is identified with or substituted for, knowledge of God. Similarly with Tillich. Firstly 'ultimate concern' or 'ground of being' is that which (as a matter of fact and not of value) is found in the last existential analysis (when one attends intensively and in depth to what it is like to 'be' and to be in relationship with other 'beings' and so when one plumbs the mystery of 'Being') just to be there in one's awareness. At this stage, 'ultimate' means the 'ground' beyond which one cannot analytically or existentially go. But secondly, 'ultimate' is taken to contain a reference to 'what really matters', 'what is felt to be finally valuable' as can be seen both from the antecedent of the idea in Schleiermacher and from the phrase 'ultimate *concern*'. Hence the ground of our being and our ultimate concern turns out to be, or to be a substitute for, God, both as the basis of the fact that anything exists at all and as the ground for being aware that existence is supremely valuable. But this type of appeal to the religious experience of the feeling of absolute dependence in order to turn the cultured despisers of religion back to what was traditionally a knowledge of, or faith in, God, can work only if all men can as a matter of fact be brought to an awareness of this feeling in themselves, and if this feeling does always have built into it a unifying sense of supreme value. And even if this were so, why should we assume that this is awareness of God unless we have other grounds for at least supposing that God exists, that all things depend on Him and that He is the supreme Good and source and fulfilment of all good?

We shall return to this when we come to discuss Tillich more fully but a few more things need to be said about Schleiermacher. In seeking to gain a hearing for the Christian religion he has turned from reason as exercised in the fields of Science and of Morality. But he has not turned to the other basis which Butler takes as the source of the Christian Religion, to revelation. This is quite understandable because the cultured men who, as such, were authoritative in their time, having already despised religion, are not going to give heed to what is essentially a *religious* appeal, viz. one to revelation. Schleiermacher, however, is convinced that he can turn from the natural endowment of reason to that of feeling, from scientific and moral experience to religious experience. This experience, uniquely and solely located in feeling, he holds to be universal to all men if only they will attend to themselves. He thus abandons the traditional objective natural theology for a theology of experienced feeling which must equally be described as natural (its basis is *ex hypothesi* common to all men as men) but which is wholly inward, subjective and arising from a particular form of self-awareness. In thus shifting the grounds for belief in God wholly to existential inwardness he shows himself truly 'modern' just as he does by his ready acceptance of the claims of 'Science' in the sphere of knowledge. In doing this he leaves all objective data in the fields of Science and Morality and allows only subjective data in the field of Religion.

It is clear enough, as I have already hinted, that there is a grave danger of this being the beginning of the end of Theism. Theism supposes that there truly exists a truly transcendent God. That is that (cf. discussion above at pp. 39 ff.) although God is so truly Other than everything else that He is not to be thought of as object-like, yet He is also to be understood as existing at least in the sense in which everything which He transcends exists. Theism holds that God 'is there' just as much as anything else which is given 'is there', however much further the doctrine of the existence of God needs necessarily (i.e. because He is God) to go. Now Schleiermacher insists that the 'being there' of God has no continuous connection with the 'being there' of the data of Science and of Morality. As I pointed out in Chapter I it is taken for granted that the data of Science and, in some sense, the data of Morality exists, i.e. 'is there'. Consequently, existence ('being there') is judged in accordance with this norm. But the existence of God is specific-ally excluded from any sort of continuity with this norm. So God (the God of Theism) must be taken for granted as not existing. Apologetic difficulties about the God of the Bible and Christianity (the cultured despisers would never grant faith any claims to objectivity on a level with science and morality) have combined with ontological difficulties about talk about such a God to produce ontological impossibility. God does not and cannot exist.

But Schleiermacher was not bothered by these possibilities because, firstly, he knew that God existed and, secondly, he did not think that such difficulties would arise. It was because he was sure that God existed that he bothered so enthusiastically with his *Speeches*, his *Christian Faith* and all his other writing and preach-ing. Moreover, his stress on the central significance of a direct awareness of God shows that, experientially, he stood within the

Biblical and Christian tradition of theism. He did not foresee the difficulties which his line of apologetic would raise because he could not distinguish his own romantic enthusiasm and sense of worshipful wonder for the world at large from the core and basis of his faith in and knowledge of God. Thus he supposed that directing men to this attitude of thankful and reverent dependence was inevitably the same thing as directing them to God. Schleiermacher believed that he was helping men to see that God exists. In fact he was describing to them what it was like for him personally to have an awareness of God. They might not share his awareness, in which case he would leave them with no grounds for believing *in* God. Or they might share his awareness but not fit it into his tradition, in which case they would have no grounds for believing that it *was* God. So, for all Schleiermacher's faith and confidence the way lay wide open towards the end of Theism. The men we now have to go on to study are the theologians, all Protestant and all stemming from Germany, who have made influential contributions in the twentieth century to the problem which Schleiermacher saw and attempted to face at the beginning of the nineteenth. Further, as we shall see, they have very largely accepted the problem as rightly posed in the way in which he saw it posed. That is, they have tended to accept the fact as a fact that religion must resign all claims on science and morality; that there is no continuity between the exercise of reason in these spheres and the awareness of God and that therefore the data which prevents the end of theism is to be found through or in the existential inwardness of faith alone. (This 'faith alone', as we shall see, is no theological accident. Was not '*sola fide*' on the banner of the Reformation?) In the last chapter we shall briefly consider not only how far these theologians have coped with Schleiermacher's problem and the problems which his solution poses but also whether the problem must be posed as he posed it.

But there must still be a postscript to this chapter. We have got half way through a book on the Debate about God without mentioning Jesus Christ. This is because we started by considering our present climate of opinion and then by being led back to consider an earlier climate of opinion and its connection with our present one. This working from the climate of opinion to the subject matter which has to be understood, put over, or maintained, in that climate is inevitable when one is considering a current debate. But, as we have already seen, to be determined in one's approach to subject matter by apologetic considerations related to a climate of opinion can be very dangerous with regard to the question of ontology and truth. Now, we have come so far without mentioning Jesus Christ because our own consideration of the climate of opinion led us on to Schleiermacher, and Schleiermacher's consideration of the climate of opinion in his time led him to tackle the question of finding a basis for the claims of religion *before* he raised the question of Jesus Christ.

For Schleiermacher, Jesus Christ is the supreme example of that immediate God-consciousness which Schleiermacher holds to be the very essence and basis of religion. As the supreme example he in some way overcomes the sin which keeps all other men from enjoying and responding to the fullness of God-consciousness themselves. He is thus in some way the source of the evocation of the perfecting of God-consciousness in others. For our purposes we do not need to be clearer as to the meaning of this nor to discuss whether, in its own terms, such an approach to Jesus Christ maintains and does justice to his uniqueness and centrality as it has usually been understood in the Christian tradition. The important point to notice is that Jesus Christ is understood, assessed and proclaimed on the basis of terms which have been evolved to meet the apologetic necessities of a particular situation. Further—and most importantly—these are the dominating and defining terms in which he is understood. This is a feature which recurs in some of the theologians we shall be considering and which is very prominent in the current debate as it is associated with Bishop Robinson and the writers with whom he has most sympathy. For Bultmann, Jesus Christ is in some way the occasion of authentic existence. For Tillich, He is the New Being (or rather the New Being is in some way in, or in association with, Him). For Robinson, He is the Man for Others. All these terms have been deliberately chosen because they are held to be determined by the ways in which men do and must think today as distinct from the mythical (and untenable) terms of the Bible or the metaphysical (and untenable) terms of the Christian tradition.

Now it is absolutely crucial to our understanding of and participation in the current debate to recognize that this type of approach from Schleiermacher onwards is deliberately and consciously maintaining that we must understand Jesus Christ in terms that are wholly congruous with the current authoritative understanding of the world. That is to say that religion has not only resigned all claims on Science and Morality but that it has also accepted the claims of Science (and perhaps of Morality) over the way in which Religion shall understand her own (allegedly unique) deliverances. This was clearly not intended by Schleiermacher and I do not think that it is intended by his various conscious or unconscious modern followers but it seems to be the logical and inevitable effect of his procedure. The result is to wholly put an end to the notion of Revelation. It is agreed and accepted that there is no source of knowledge (no way of getting on to 'what is there') other than the procedures which are acceptable to Science as Science. Traditionally it was supposed that it was Jesus Christ who, in the last analysis, had the last word on one's understanding of the ultimate reality of and in the world. (To be a Christian meant that one believed this to be true and therefore to be committed to attempting to act, live and hope accordingly. Jesus was believed to be 'Lord'—a term with a mythological background but with the logical effect which I have just been outlining.) Today it is being supposed (in practice) that one's understanding of the world must have the last word about one's understanding of the ultimate reality or true meaning of Jesus. *Part* of the 'debate about God' is therefore bound to be a pretty agonizing debate among Christians about whether, if things are clearly put this way round, one is entitled to retain the designation Christian at all. A by-product of this part of the debate has been the attempt in some quarters to imply that all, say, deeply morally committed atheists are 'really' Christians, just as all, say, truly modern Christians are 'really' atheists. This may be honest (the debate is about whether it is honest or not) but to many, both atheists and Christians, it looks irritatingly dishonest. The atheist sees no reason to cling to the uniqueness of Jesus which would justify the continuing use of the term 'Christian' and the Christian does not find a sufficient appreciation of the uniqueness of Jesus which he associates with Christian commitment.

However, as we are concerned with outlining the terms of the debate and not with settling it, it is sufficient to draw attention to the way in which the debate does focus on Jesus and to point out that even if it is held that the more traditional atheist and Christian are right in their assessment of the situation then the question, from the Christian point of view, is 'How do we get on to this uniqueness of Jesus and how do we know that the uniqueness refers to something that is 'really there' when we do get on to it?'. In other words the debate is still about data and whether it is really data which counts for evidence of existence or of 'being there'. Schleiermacher raised in a new way the question of God and, in effect, asked 'What is that area of human experiencing in which awareness of God is to be found?' He thought it right and necessary to raise that question before he got on to the question of Jesus, although he raised it as a Christian, i.e. with the assumption that as a matter of fact Jesus is at the practical centre of the answer to the question. Even if it is argued (as we shall see it is argued by some of the theologians we are going on to consider) that the only possible procedure is to begin from the question about Jesus, there will still be the question as to how Jesus is, and is known to be, central and crucial to the question about God.

Thus, Schleiermacher has either posed or caused all the main questions in the debate about God, the attempted answers to which we are about to go on to consider. And he is so important and influential because he has raised the whole matter with a very full awareness of the modern situation with regard to authority and the authoritative man. He is fully aware of *and* appreciative of the prestige of Science with regard to the determining of the question as to what is 'really there'. So we have a debate which turns on the question of data and on the appeal to experience rather than on the citation of authorities which are *above* the debate, whether they are authorities of reason or of revelation. Now this is a debate which, if I may dare to put it so, ought to be thoroughly congenial to a believer in the God portrayed in the Bible. For this God is nothing if not involved in the affairs of His world and His people, and His method of revelation might well be crudely described as that of 'getting Himself experienced'. But it must finally be noted that Schleiermacher has set the terms of the debate in a very unbalanced way. In abandoning the old appeal to reason and revelation, as both related and yet different sources of genuine information, he has logically put God at the mercy of man. For we can only feel about God and only know about Science and Morality. Knowing and doing will surely define and delimit whether and how far feeling is 'about' any-thing (at least as far as possible and with Freud helping us). God is destined to become the affective tone of our scientific and moral dealings with reality. All theology, as Feuerbach said, is anthro-pology. God is out although godly attitudes remain in. And if we ask why they remain in, the answer might be, 'Because God does put Himself at the mercy of man and yet somehow does not leave Himself without witness'. *This* answer will have to be considered when we come to Bonhoeffer. And then we shall also have tiresomely to ask how, if God does this, we can possibly know or even guess that He does it. At any rate the scales seem loaded against God, and before we come to Bonhoeffer's answer that Jesus makes it clear that this is how God has always wanted it, we must try and see the outlines of the ways in which Bultmann and Barth, Brunner and Tillich have tackled the problem. After we have considered where Bonhoeffer may be supposed to stand we will then, in a final chapter, consider whether the problem must be posed just as Schleiermacher posed it, and therefore whether our resources for considering the question of the end of theism are confined to those set before us by these influential Germans.

We shall allow our discussion to take its shape from the four questions which seem to be involved in or raised by Schleiermacher's discussion. These are the question of data, the question of experience, the question of the attitude to and role of Jesus Christ and the question of the world or of the place and prestige of Science. As we pursue this inquiry we may well find that the question of God is to be approached through the questions of man, of Jesus and of the world. And, finally, that *the* debate about God is whether the first question, that of God, turns out to be dissolved into the other three or whether the other three find their distinctive and only answer and fulfilment in the answer to the first. Is 'God' the *name* for the meaning which we find in man, Jesus and the world or does the world, man and Jesus *have* a meaning precisely because God is God—independently and in his own right?

Chapter Three

BULTMANN AND THE 'BUT' OF FAITH

WE HAVE FOUND that the debate about God takes the form of a quest for data about God and experience of God. I have just suggested (p. 53 above) that the shape which Schleiermacher gave to this quest was that of looking for the answer to the question 'What is that area of human experiencing in which awareness of God is to be found?' Bultmann's answer to this question can best be understood for our purposes as having three sections or layers. (1) Nothing at all can be found in our experience of the world (i.e. the experiencing which goes with, is part of, or makes up Science has no significance with regard to the question of God. Or rather—has only a negative significance. (See below) (2) It is the question of existence which puts a man on to the question of God. Indeed the question of my existence *is the same thing* as the question of God. (This is a personal and existential question and not a scientific and objective question—and these two types of question are radically opposed to one another or, at least, in no way overlap). (3) BUT even the question of existence (strictly of *my* existence, for such questions can only be particular and not general) cannot put me on to God apart from FAITH. Hence the reference in the title of the chapter to the 'BUT' of faith. We must now endeavour to see what is involved in each of these three sections.

Bultmann wholeheartedly agrees with Schleiermacher that religion resigns and must resign all claims on Science. The modern scientific world-view, which is *the* view of modern man, takes it for granted that the Universe is a closed system with its own independent laws and patterns which are or can be open to discovery by observation and investigation. Any trustworthy observation which is made of any happening or any pattern of happenings anywhere in the Universe is bound to be able, eventually, to be fitted in to a pattern of explanation and understanding which embraces the whole of the data so far observed. This pattern of scientific understanding and explanation is, of course, constantly changing as new observations and new understandings require. But this flexibility is precisely its strength and guarantees its completeness as a *method* of understanding and explanation. The method can and does cope with everything observable without having recourse to any 'explanation' *outside* the type of observable things and happenings or *different from* the type of patterns of explanation which constitute this method. The observable world has and can have no room for happenings which are caused by anything which is not part of the observable world. Of course that which will enable some observed happenings to be fitted into explanatory patterns has not yet been observed but it is certainly observable. Gaps indicate observations not yet made, not opportunities for the insertion or explanations of a wholly different (e.g. supernatural) sort. And what applies to the happenings which are the subject of the observations of Science applies also to the events which are the subject of the investigations of History. In so far as it is proper to talk about historical causes or patterns of events in history, these causes and patterns will always be of the sort which fall *within* that which can be historically investigated. Gaps in understanding and explanation will be much greater here in the nature of the case. Sufficient data is rarely available or likely to become available but the gaps simply represent this and cannot be construed as opportunities, still less as justifications, for the insertion into historical events of supra-historical causes.

It is from this diagnosis of modern man's approach to happenings in the world and his acceptance of that diagnosis that there arises Bultmann's famous concern for 'demythologizing'. A myth is a form of portraying happenings in the world as empirical events with transcendent causes. A mythical approach to reality is one which takes it for granted that observable and recordable events may be literally described and understood as having not only scientific and historical causes but also as having divine or supernatural causes and that these last are causes in the same sense and with the same type of effect as the former. A notable and notorious example of mythical thinking would be the Virgin Birth of Jesus in the commonly accepted sense of the understanding that the infant would not have been born (an historical happening related normally to scientifically understandable causes) unless the divine cause of virginal conception were operative within the nexus of scientific and historical happenings—and, indeed, *as* a scientific and historical event.

Such a mythical approach to reality is quite out of the question for modern man. Scientific and historical causes are all he knows about, all he can know about—and all there is to know about as far as the natural (i.e. given) universe and the events of history are concerned. Talk which interweaves supernatural events with natural ones (e.g. takes miracles as both 'miracles' i.e. divinely caused, and events i.e. ordinarily observable) or intersperses historical happenings with happenings with a supra- or extra-historical source (e.g. supposes that an historical personage 'comes down from Heaven' or is in a literally descriptive sense 'the Son of God') is always mythological and cannot be understood or meaningfully made use of by modern man. This means that practically the whole of the Bible is strictly non-sense today. But Bultmann (like Schleiermacher before him) is a Christian believer. He does not for one moment suppose that the Bible *is* nonsense or that there is no longer any meaning or point in the

Christian Gospel. Rather he holds that it is urgently necessary to demythologize the Biblical way of looking at the world and the traditional way of understanding and presenting the Christian Gospel so that modern men may once again hear it as Gospel and not as nonsense. What this programme of demythologizing is and how it can have any basis or claim to validity can be seen only when we have considered the two further sections of Bultmann's reply to the question about that area of human experiencing in which there is to be encountered data about God.

Bultmann accepts that as a cause God is out of the Universe as known to Science and History. Indeed, he accepts and stresses the fact that God is out of the Universe. He repeatedly talks of the absolute hiddenness of God and of how the Universe gives no sign whatever of His presence or existence. How then can Bultmann possibly do anything other than acquiesce in the complete end and disappearance of all theism, including the cessation of all talk about God? He avoids the end of theism, indeed, he believes that he points the way to the only true and valid theism by making a radical distinction between empirical experience and existential experience. The meaning of this distinction can be understood when one passes from asking questions about the world to asking questions about existence. Questions about the world are questions about the objects, events and happenings given in and to experience. Answers are arrived at by generalizing and systematizing arrangements of objective, experienced data which enable one to understand, explain and manipulate the world. The experience which is the way one receives this data is 'empirical' i.e. experience of objects and happenings as objects and happenings outside oneself. But existential questions do not arise out of this type of objective, empirical experience but out of the subjective experience of what it is like to be, and what is involved in being, an experiencing subject. *The* question of existence is 'What is it like for me to be me and what does it mean for me to be me?' or to put it more generally (in so far as such a question can be put generally at all) 'how does man desire to understand himself and how is he to understand himself?' This question can be *put* generally but it can only be *understood* individually i.e. in so far as I am aware of the questioning, concern and anxiety which I have about being me. Bultmann holds that there is literally all the difference in the world between these two types of question and that you cannot answer questions of the existential type by the help of data which is relevant to questions of the empirical type. No amount of data about the world can settle the question of what it means to be me or assuage my concern over what it is like to be me. Indeed, the existential effect of data about the world is to threaten me in my existence, to make me see how much I am at the mercy of chance, how under the limitations of systems entirely indifferent to me and how inexorably my existence is under the sentence of death.

But in facing the question of what it is like to be me I find also that I am a being who has to take decisions and make moral choices and that I have longings for freedom and fulfilment, particularly in relation to and with other human beings. The question of existence, therefore, is whether I am simply a determined object in the closed system of the world or whether I am a subject who can be set free from the threatening determinations of the world for freedom and fulfilment as a person with persons. And *this* question, Bultmann argues, is the question of God, i.e. the question of the existence of God as the transcendent existential possibility, not part of the world as a system, which gives fulfilment to personal living. But the question is not known to be the question of God. It is known, or rather experienced, as the question of the threat to my existence and of the unfulfilledness of my existence. It cannot be known as the question of God because there is no evidence in the world for the existence of God. (The world for modern man is inescapably a closed system—*vide supra.*) Moreover, looked at in the way which is natural to and inevitable for any modern man, Biblical talk about 'God' (NB the inverted commas) cannot be relevantly brought to bear on his question of existence because it is this mythological talk about 'God' as, at least partly, an object in and active in the world. And modern man, in his existential plight, knows that such talk is nonsense and, as such, of course irrelevant to his problem. We, therefore, (for we are all modern men whatever stratagems of escapism we may resort to to deny the reality of our state) cannot meaningfully and existentially put together our understanding of the question of our existence and any talk about 'God' (we cannot get rid of the inverted commas).

But this is where we come to the third layer in Bultmann's denial of the end of theism. While we cannot put together our awareness of the question of existence and any talk about God we may find that the question is answered in such a way in our particular existential awareness that we are at one and the same time aware that the question was the question of God and that it has a positive answer. That is to say that we may be existentially aware that we have faith in God. This awareness is experienced as a deliverance from our inauthentic existence into authentic existence. The inauthenticity of our threatened, limited and anxious existence is replaced by the authenticity of freedom from the past (the determinism of events in the world and the inevitability of the purely historical series of events which have hitherto composed our personal history) and openness for the future (which is no longer experienced as the threat of blind chance and final meaninglessness). This is an awareness that we have been delivered by love for love. The deliverance could not have come from within the world or from within ourselves. It is the 'nevertheless' of Faith which assures us that, despite the empirical features of the world and despite our own existential awareness that we are unable to be ourselves, *nevertheless* we are set free from the world and from ourselves with the possibility of being our true selves. This does not give us a new systematic approach to the world and our life in it. We do not have a world-view to substitute for the world-view of Science. That continues to be the only possible world-view. But in each moment of our encounter with the world and of our life in the world we are able to have faith which consists in being aware that it is not the possibilities of the world which determine the question of our existence but the transcendent, the wholly other, possibility of God.

Thus Bultmann's answer to the question 'What is that area of human experiencing in which awareness of God is to be found?' is—Faith. There is no data in the world which can put you on to God but there is faith. But why should we call this experience of deliverance 'faith' and why should we associate it with God? This is where we come back to the Bible and come to consider the role of Jesus. The Bible exists as evidence that God has constantly acted to allow men this possibility of authentic existence which is faith. Men have interpreted this existential act of God as if it were empirical and therefore mythologized it. That is to say they have spoken and written as if the acts of God were concrete interventions in history and productive of scientific-like causes in changing or producing situations. But the existential and demythologized understanding of this is that God has always and only acted in his *Word* whereby men who have heard this Word have been set free for authentic existence for God and for their fellows. There has been no act of God *as* an historical event but only (although this is transcendent deliverance enough!) the hearing of God's Word *in* historical events—which have, on the historical and scientific level, been historically and scientifically determined by their own autonomous historical and scientific causes. What finally and decisively makes plain that God acts in this way in His Word is Jesus.

Here we must dovetail into the exposition a brief reference to the influence of Biblical criticism on the way in which Bultmann seeks to answer the question about God. He belongs to the most radical school of New Testament critics. He believes that he is justified on strictly critical and literary grounds in taking a very sceptical view of the value of the Gospels as sources for historical evidence. He would, I think, maintain that this view of the Gospel records is required on objective grounds independent of judgments or presuppositions about the necessity for or validity of 'demythologization'. The matter is very complex and it is exceedingly difficult to be clear how far Bultmann makes up his mind that a particular piece of the Gospel record is unhistorical because it is mythological (and therefore could not have happened) and how far he decides on quite other grounds that the passage is unhistorical (i.e. does not recount something which happened) and therefore must have a demythologized meaning if it is to have any meaning for us at all. But, in any case, it is clear that there is bound to be a very close interaction between the discovery that a set of texts can not be straightforwardly relied on for literal historical evidence and a conviction that the sort of things which the texts are describing are not to be taken as straightforwardly historical statements in any case.

To take again the example of the Virgin Birth. A comparative study of the relevant texts of the New Testament, once it is freed from the presupposition that all the texts must both be literally true and be literally reconcilable, will soon raise questions as to whether the New Testament taken as a whole and taken solely in its own terms obliges us to accept the Virgin Birth as an historical fact. Neither Mark nor John feel any need to mention it. Very possibly one or two passages in those gospels may be taken to presuppose the contrary and passages in Paul seem most naturally to suggest the same (e.g. that Jesus was born naturally in the house of David). It is then noticed that the Birth Narratives in both Matthew and Luke look exceedingly like introductory explanatory stories put as prefaces to the historical narrative and so on. (The argument is well known—and can be argued the other way.) Whatever decision one may come to about the weight of the evidence, it is decisively clear that one cannot (save as an act of sheer and unsupported faith which goes in the face of what would normally be taken as decisive evidence) take the mere fact of appearance in a biblical narrative as evidence for historicity, and conversely one has also established the fact that the Bible makes use of unhistorical material for the purposes of conveying its message (i.e. that the authors of the biblical material do). This will be a great source of encouragement to someone who already believes that the Virgin Birth *must* be a piece of mythological narrative in any case.

Conversely, there is a point which is of the highest significance for the whole debate about God and which is relevant to the approach of all the theologians we are considering. It is this. If, as a modern man, you are having the greatest difficulty with various biblical notions like miracle, God intervening from 'outside' history to bring about saving acts in history and so on, you will now find that the Bible as unique but also uniquely authoritative evidence that this sort of thing does happen has now let you down. You cannot now set against the evidence of what you find normally thinkable what the Bible clearly and decisively requires you to think. Even if you are prepared to make an act of faith and use intervention language as literally true it is now by no means clear that the New Testament unambiguously requires you to believe in the particular intervention of the Virgin Birth. And where does this process stop? Wherever it does, it will have become clear that the Bible has ceased to be an independent and self-contained source of evidence as to what is to be judged as possibly historical. The most that can be done is to put together what seems to be the most reasonable modern view of what is historical with what it seems right to make of the Bible. What has happened is that *both* of Bishop Butler's bases for the Christian Faith have proved inadequate. Reason gives you no guaranteed data about God. But neither does Revelation, if your source of Revelation is the statements of the Bible. This is the position which the development of Biblical criticism throughout the nineteenth century has brought about. (A very clear statement of the history of this can be read in Stephen Neil's—*The Interpretation of the New Testament 1861–1961*, Oxford.) Now Protestants have tended not to be very concerned about the collapse of Reason in relation to awareness of God. But the collapse of the Bible, at least in its old role as supplier of guaranteed data about God, has seemed disastrous.

But Bultmann refuses to find it so. He is quite convinced that the Bible has so collapsed and, as I have said, he takes a very sceptical view of the historical value of the New Testament. (Far more sceptical than, I believe, the consensus of scholarship will eventually allow.) But this is theologically excellent for it makes it absolutely clear that salvation, the liberating awareness of authentic existence which comes as the gracious act of God is *by faith alone*—the Reformation principle which the Reformers did not sufficiently radically apply. This is the faith of Jesus, the faith which was aroused in the first disciples through their association with Jesus and which is aroused in subsequent generations by the preaching of faithful men whose testimony to faith, proceeding from faith, becomes the occasion of the awakening of faith in others. We cannot get back to the historicity of the events which gave rise to the New Testament because the New Testament record is the result of and the portrayal of faith and that by first century men. Hence everything is mythologically described to convey existential awareness that through Jesus they had received newness of life, i.e. authentic existence. But it does not matter that we cannot get back to historicity for God is not in historicity.

c

He is solely in faith. And this is what is presented to us in the New Testament. With this understanding we can be clear that Jesus was the occasion of this saving faith and by sifting the faithful (and therefore unhistorical) records of his life we can see that he was the occasion of this faith because he himself lived this faith out completely. He triumphed over all the historical circumstances of his life, including his death and passion, because he always lived by faith alone and was therefore always free from the past and present of sinful men and open to God's future fulfilment. The disciples' discovery and conviction of this existential and faithful triumph of Jesus is their conviction of the Resurrection whereby they too became aware that there was open to them Jesus' freedom, in the present, from the past, for the future of God. And from their experience they proclaimed the same Word as Jesus had proclaimed, namely the word of the deliverance of God which makes men aware of the availability of the possibility of authentic existence. And because they thought mythologically they identified Jesus as the Word. In this they were right in so far as Jesus, having demonstrated the actuality of authentic existence in the world up to and beyond death, has demonstrated this Word of God in a final and decisive manner. But in so far as they took Jesus as historically, literally and concretely the Word of God (and thus laid the foundations of classical Trinitarian and Christological metaphysics) they were simply mythologizing their existential insight. Now we have to be freed of this unbelievable mythology and metaphysics so that we may once again hear the Word in our existential situation and receive the deliverance into authentic existence which is faith in God given through Jesus.

Thus the end of theism is precluded as long as there is the faithful proclamation of the Word of God in Jesus and as long as men hear this Word in such a way that Faith is awakened in them. But this Faith is an 'as if not'. That is to say it has no basis in the world of Science and of History and it is not guaranteed or even suggested by the Bible simply read as such. It is discovered, understood and found credible only when it happens. It is sheer miracle, indeed the only miracle and it is the gracious act of the wholly transcendent God, who is truly transcendent because He is in no sense whatever 'in' the events of this world as happening, event or object. Bultmann denies very firmly that because we are aware of God only and solely in faith, therefore 'God' is really only a name for my faith. He believes that thus to subjectivize the existential awareness of deliverance into authentic existence is to wholly fail to do justice to its existential nature. The deliverance is transcendent and of God. Thus he will not agree with those of his 'followers' who insist that he ought logically to demythologize also the notion of the deliverance by an act of God. This is an existential act and not an empirical act. It is not therefore an historical act and so it is not speaking mythologically to say that God acts in this way. He quite understands that people should not find such an act credible. It is incredible until you are existentially aware of it.

Thus the data for the existence of God *is* the experience of Faith. It arises in connection with the preaching of the Word which is the Word about Jesus and the Word of Jesus and we are to be clear that the world has nothing to do with this and can have nothing to do with it. Such is Bultmann's position on the four points in the debate about God which we found arising out of our consideration of Schleiermacher. Bultmann accepts Schleiermacher's position about the absolute autonomy of Science but thinks it useless to rely on a substitute for natural knowledge of God like the feeling of absolute dependence. None the less he agrees with Schleiermacher that it is only in actual experience that any talk about God can be meaningful, and he works out radically that notion which I believed to be touched upon in Schleiermacher and which I said was an essential part of the Christian tradition, namely that the decisive knowledge of God must be direct and self-authenticating. For Bultmann, awareness of God is not only completely self-authenticating but also quite unrelated to any other awareness. It is for this reason that his position has been described as that of 'Radical Subjectivity'. 'Subjectivity' because the basis of my awareness of God is my faith and 'radical' because it is both unconnected with anything else and yet wholly decisive. We may perhaps ask whether this sheer miracle of faith with no connection with anything else in the world can prevent the end of Theism. The answer presumably is that if God is God and if He acts like that then it will. Which raises the question whether the Biblical and Christian evidence is that He does act like that. But that is a question to be touched on at various points in the book, not least in the last chapter and then to be taken into the debate at large.

What has to be noted is that Bultmann is making a very power-ful attempt, which he believes to be wholly in line with the decisive insight of Protestant Christianity, to confront the world's assertion of the end of theism with a full awareness of the way Science has affected the manner and the possibilities of men's thinking. Further, it is to be noted that whatever younger contributors to the debate about God may do he himself does not believe that his method of demythologizing removes the scandal from Christianity. He believes it to be the way of bring-ing the scandal to bear on modern man and he is quite clear that the Word of the Gospel is at the same time, and indeed, first, a word of judgment. The demand of faith is both a paradox and a stumbling-block to modern men just as it has been to all men. So Bultmann remains offensively divisive, as the philosopher Jaspers has not been slow to point out.

Finally, reference must be made to Bultmann's understanding of Faith as decision. The act of Faith which *is* our awareness of God (not *in which* we are aware of God) is an act of commitment, a decision, not an act of knowing. Faith is the decision not to take the world and history as all there is but to be open to the future and the transcendent possibilities of God. It is a decision which is renewed in every 'moment', that is every time we are existentially challenged either to acquiesce in the determinism of the world or to stand firm for the openness of God. In every such moment when we decide for the openness of God we are aware that that possibility is real and authentic for us and therefore we have faith in God and this is our awareness of Him. But Bultmann is very careful to maintain that we do not *know* God as a Given who transcends the moments by spanning them and linking them together. This, he holds, would be to turn God into an object related to the empirical series i.e. to mythologize Him, make Him incredible, and, indeed, as within the historical series not worth believing in. So we see that although Bultmann is anxious to stress the role of direct authentication in awareness of God he cannot agree with such as Augustine and Anselm that such direct awareness could be knowledge. That is why Bultmann's position on the transcendence of God can seem either unclear or else illogical for his own understanding of things. Is God 'there' or not? Presumably the answer is—in so far as 'there' is a place word —God is not 'there'. In so far as we are delivered in to authentic existence by that which is beyond our experiences and our hopes God is—if not 'there'—certainly God. In any case Bultmann agrees with Schleiermacher in agreeing with the scientists that knowledge is only of things which are 'there' and that this applies only to that which can be the object of scientific investigation.

But despite his denial that 'God' can be reduced to the name of my faith Bultmann's talk of faith as decision does add weight to this suspicion for it seems that my faith in God is my decision to choose God and not the determinism of the world. In so far as this is so, then it would seem that the continuing of theism depends on some men choosing God. Karl Barth, to whom we must now pass, would hold that this is the supreme blasphemy. The continuing of theism depends on the fact that God continues to choose some men.

[Those who wish to understand Bultmann more fully might find the following reading helpful:—

Jesus Christ and Mythology (SCM Paperback)

Introduction by S. Ogden to *Existence and Faith*—shorter writings of Rudolf Bultmann selected, translated and introduced by Schubert M. Ogden. (Hodder & Stoughton)

The Crisis in Belief and *The Question of Natural Revelation* in *Essays Philosophical and Theological*. (SCM Press)

Bultmann replies to his critics in *Kerygma and Myth* Vol. I (S.P.C.K.)

And the other essays in the books listed—but I have listed the articles in the order in which I think an introductory reading would be most helpful.]

Chapter Four

BARTH AND THE GIVENNESS OF THE WORD

KARL BARTH'S REPLY to the main question we are pursuing, viz. whence do we get data which makes us aware of the being and activity of God, is quite uncompromising, and to anyone in a debating frame of mind, at first sight at least, quite shatteringly unsatisfactory. His reply, in effect, is 'From whom do you suppose? *From God.* For whence else could it possibly come? And do not suppose either that *you* (or I or any other man) can "get it". God gives it or you will not have it at all'.

We may eventually accept this answer and thereby, as theists, believe that we have a satisfactory account of, and justification for, our faith or, as atheists, hold that we were right in believing that there is no evidence for God and that *we* are justified *in our* faith, or we may eventually reject it in its uncompromising starkness. But whatever we eventually do, we ought first to make an attempt to appreciate the type of reasons and reasonings which lead up to this answer.

Some of the people who plunge fairly dogmatically into the debate about God may be surprisingly oblivious to the development of the history of ideas in European thought which lay behind Schleiermacher and stretch out after him. But Barth is clearly an authoritative surveyor of these developments and the understanding of the Christian position which he works out is worked out with a very carefully maintained awareness of the developments. His system is no ill-considered response to a panic-situation which has suddenly burst upon him in his unawareness.

71

Secondly, if it can be held that theologians can have virtue as such (even despite the fact that, possibly, they are entirely on the wrong tack) then Barth is clearly a superb theologian. He is familiar with an amazing amount of the whole Christian tradition. He clearly searches the scriptures with devoutness, insight and a highly questioning energy. And however baffling and infuriating he may be to those who have not acquired the taste, those who are prepared to go round and round a question with him cannot do so for long before they find themselves confronted with a new and illuminating insight or at least a new and fruitful question.

But it must be admitted that you do have to acquire the taste, that many people cannot do it when they try and that many do not have the time to try. Barth is a theologian's theologian (*now*—doubtless in the nineteen twenties and thirties he played a great part under God in keeping alive the soul of the whole Confessing Church in Germany. But we shall come to that). Therefore, I must bring the dreadful wrath of all Barthians about my head and say that I do not myself believe that Karl Barth is of very much use to us *in the heat of the present debate*. Indeed, I believe that some of the aspects of the present debate (not least Bonhoeffer's distinctive contribution to it) arise largely because Barth's attempted (and magnificently attempted) answer to the question about the whence of data about God does not come off either theologically or pragmatically. It suffices for Barthian addicts only and it hardly gets through to the pew or the discussion group, let alone to the outsider (although as we shall see, this last point is taken for granted by the system). None the less one must surely pay a genuine and deeply respectful tribute to him as a man and as a theologian. If he is of little use *in* the debate, he is of the greatest use as preparation for the debate and as a source of judgment and renewal for returning to the debate.

His immense knowledge of the Bible, of Christian Theology and of the history of Philosophy is put at the service of one thing

—the knowledge of God. This is done with such humanity, humour and serenity that I for one cannot doubt that he knows God and that it is indeed God whom he knows. (Anyone who is suffering from taking the debate—not too seriously for it cannot be taken too seriously—but too solemnly and in too anxious a spirit could take as a tonic Barth's discussion of Bultmann, published in *Kerygma and Myth*, Volume II. The humour and the hard-hitting reveal a man who is free for and free in the debate and who may well, therefore, be believed to be in touch with something which —? the One who?—transcends the debate.) Further, although he is convinced that knowledge of the world is absolutely useless as far as knowledge of God goes and although he lays the greatest stress on the radical sinfulness of man, there is no gloom or negation in his approach to the world or to man. He believes in infinite possibilities for man and he affirms the glory of creation. Of this last aspect of his thought his splendid enthusiasm for the music of Mozart is peculiarly attractive evidence. It is the witness of the man and the spirit of his arguing rather than the form of his system or the strict content of his arguments which seem to me to be invaluable to us in the debate. In all his writing, although he goes on *and on* (!) it is the looking *in* which is impressive—the looking inwards to the Presence to whose judgment everything is to be submitted and from whose revelation everything is to be understood. Barth reminds the would-be debater about God at least of something of what the godness of God would be like if God were God. I would believe far more than this. That Barth stands in the succession of those, such as Augustine and Anselm, whom Barth himself so seeks to follow, who speak of God in such a way that the spiritual fumblers among us are encouraged to believe that there is indeed a God to speak of.

But we are debating, not believing, and we must proceed from the point that Barth reminds us of what the godness of God would be like if God were God. Here it is important to be aware that the impetus to Barth's radical theologizing had a moral, social and political source. He was finally jerked out of any share in the Liberal tradition (where the Schleiermacher stream had got to by the end of the nineteenth century) by the acquiescence of the theologians in the movement to war in 1914. 'One day in early August 1914 stands out in my personal memory as a black day. Ninety-three German intellectuals impressed public opinion by their proclamation in support of the war policy of Wilhelm II and his counsellors. Among these intellectuals I discovered to my horror almost all of my theological teachers whom I had greatly venerated. In despair over what this indicated about the signs of the time I suddenly realized that I could no longer follow either their ethics and dogmatics or their understanding of the Bible and of history. For me at least, 19th century theology no longer held any future.' (*Evangelical Theology in the Nineteenth Century* in *The Humanity of God*—p. 14). Later, in the nineteen thirties when the National Socialists were producing the 'German-Christian' movement and seeking to dragoon the church for their own nationalist purposes, Barth was to find even more sharply that the Christian whose theology came to terms with the current thinking of the world on the world's own terms likewise came to terms with the government on its own terms and that this was a betrayal of Christianity and humanity. What the needs of the time and the authentic biblical and Christian tradition alike demanded was to stand radically over against the conformities and patterns of contemporary thinking. True theology is 'against the stream'.

It may be held that the starkness of the situation in 1914 and 1934 demanded a corresponding starkness of theological witness, and to some extent Barth would seem to agree with this but his discovery, his shock and his stand draws our attention to the inescapable even if uncomfortable fact that at the heart of the biblical tradition of theism, knowledge of God is intimately bound up with discovering the judgment of God and that one of the most important elements in an awareness of the otherness and transcendence of God is a sense of his holiness which makes us see the world and ourselves in a wholly different light. Whether a projected super-ego is really a plausible explanation for the radical and creative judgments on individuals and societies which lie at the heart of the biblical and Christian tradition of theism is a question worthy of debate and remains so despite the way in which Christians, like others, ignore these judgments. Conversely, to play down the element of judgment and therefore scandal in this tradition by over-concentration on what is otherwise (i.e. apart from the tradition) thinkable may well be to suppress one of the most important types of evidence for the objective truth of the tradition. Whatever we may be led to decide is the truth here, Barth felt obliged to challenge head on the unholy alliance of Schleiermacher and the scientists (or men of modern culture) to which Bultmann also acceded, in taking it for granted that knowledge has as its objects only that which is or can be the object of science.

Over against the objects known to science there is the Object known to faith. This object is God who, being God, wholly dictates both the very existence of faith (hence the importance of the doctrine of Election—see below) and the shape and content of faith. It is clean contrary to the existence and being of the living and true God to whom the Bible bears witness to suppose that we can arrive at any conception of his existence, let alone his character, from any concepts of our own. We are men and not God and must never forget the infinite qualitative difference between God and man. Anything which fits into human moulds of thought or is derived from human thinking, and therefore moulded by human concepts, cannot possibly be God. God does not fit into anything whatever. He is wholly free of all 'fittingness' and all 'fitting in'. He is God and therefore free, sovereign, transcendent and, in the strictest sense, inconceivable. Since this is so, to attempt to talk about God as Schleiermacher did by starting from some general human concepts (e.g. 'absolute dependence') is to guarantee that you will not be talking about God at all. Start from what men find thinkable and you can never get to God. At best, although God is out, godly attitudes may remain in, but since they have no truth neither will they have any strength, so that when any truly testing crisis arises they will be sucked in to the prevailing human climate of opinion. This approach from the human end has effectively 'immunized the concept of revelation'. And where there is no revelation of God there is no knowledge of God or contact with God.

But the 'revelation of God' must mean the 'revelation which God gives of Himself'. No human thoughts can go from man to God. We can know God, therefore, only if God enables our human thinking to be informed by God's thinking about Himself. And this is precisely what He does do in and through His Word. And this is not a theoretical answer to the problem of data about God any more than the concept of God's Word is a theoretical concept, because God's Word is the historical Jesus Christ. Barth does not believe himself to be making up a system to cope with the problem of faith in God in the modern age. He is concerned simply to unfold what is involved in the givenness of Jesus Christ. And what is involved here is the sheer miracle of God's giving himself to be the man Jesus Christ.

God is God. He is, therefore, absolutely free to do whatever He wishes. As His thoughts are not our thoughts we cannot tell in advance what He wishes to do. Nor, even when He has done something can we recognize that God has done it unless He gives us that recognition. For if we were able to recognize something or someone as the action of God on our own this would mean once again that we were fitting God into our categories. And this is impossible. Therefore from first to last we are wholly dependent

upon God's giving us recognition of Him as He gives us knowledge of Himself and on His giving us knowledge of Himself as He
grants us recognition. The knowledge of God is, therefore, sheer
miracle from God to man given straight down from above. The
centre of this miracle is the God-given recognition that Jesus is
the Christ, that is that He is the fulfilment of God's Word
witnessed to by the Old Testament because He is Himself personally that Word. The Christian Gospel is preached because Jesus
Christ has been recognized to be the Word of God and the content
of the Gospel *is* Jesus Christ as the Word of God. Here men are,
by God (the Holy Spirit), brought up against the truth and
reality of God in historical and concrete form (Jesus Christ, the
Word of God Incarnate) so that they may know the true God and
be truly related to that Truth. The witness to the Word of God
Incarnate is the written Word, the Scriptures which exist in their
sheer matter-of-fact givenness, just as the historical Jesus Christ
did in his. There are no general, theoretical and therefore humanly
recognizable reasons why *these* Scriptures should be the Word of
God written, any more than there are why *this* man Jesus should be
the Word of God incarnate. The fact is that they are so and this fact
is known as fact because it is in and through the Scriptures and in
and through Jesus Christ that men are convinced of the knowledge
of God and convicted by the knowledge of God. There is no
way into this knowledge of God unless God Himself chooses to
give you this knowledge and if He chooses to give you this
knowledge you know that you have it. Hence there is the closest
possible connection between the knowledge of God and God's
'election'. God, since He is God and therefore completely free,
must be understood as having chosen to give the knowledge of
God to those who have it. Once again, it is not for those who are
chosen to attempt to fit this choosing into some theoretical
pattern as if men could 'round off' the ways of God. It is simply
their expression of their understanding that they do have the

knowledge of God. And to this they must respond without blasphemously turning this understanding into a doctrine of privilege or of salvation for themselves alone. All along men must respond obediently in both thought and act to what God has given and develop their understanding from there. The godness of God cannot possibly permit anything else. Everything must start from God, that is from what He has chosen to make known of Himself, that is from Jesus Christ His Word.

Barth strenuously maintains that although this knowledge of God is a purely miraculous and gracious gift of God—or, rather just *because* it is such, it is truly knowledge, something fully rational and objective. For God imparts His Word which is supremely rational and it is a true impartation and therefore fully objective. Theology, therefore, is a rational science independent of all other sciences but totally dependent on its proper object, God, and subject to the methods dictated by the nature of that Object. In relation to our questions about data, experience, the world and Jesus, Barth's position is that the data of Theology is the Word of God given by God Himself, that this is primarily Jesus Christ, experienced as the Incarnate Word, and secondarily the Word of God experienced by the grace of God through Holy Scripture, the written Word. The world contributes nothing to this data but is wholly dependent on this data for its full understanding and use. Barth has seen that Schleiermacher's admission that religion has *no* claims on the subject matter of Science in the form in which it was made led inevitably to the surrender of Christianity to the claims of current, allegedly scientifically based world-views. While accepting that religion and science have no source of knowledge in common he sets up the given Word of God as a source of knowledge wholly independent of all other sources and having the last and independent word on the true evaluation of all other knowledge. It is easy to see, therefore, why, when Barth passes from being a prophet to being a systematizer he becomes a theologian's theologian. He restores autonomy to Theology by putting it in splendid isolation.

This splendid isolation also allows Barth to scout round the difficult question of the historical status of the Gospel accounts to which we drew attention in discussing Bultmann (see pp. 63 ff.). Your knowledge of Jesus Christ as the Word of God does not depend in any way on what you can gather from the Gospel records as being true of the historical Jesus but entirely on God's act of grace in causing you to know that Jesus Christ is His Word. You know that the New Testament is God's Word written because through it God has revealed to you Jesus Christ as His Word. Therefore you can make use of the New Testament as the vehicle of God's Word without any further concern about the historicity of any particular part. Here again we have a circle where the believer need have no further concern about history and where the unbeliever's concern about history can do him no good. This seems a very odd result for a system which claims to make the Incarnation so absolutely central. If God were really *in* history then it might well seem that He would be exposed to the risks of history and that faith in Him would be exposed to those risks also. Barth certainly talks of God's 'incognito' (He is truly man and therefore not recognizable as God in Jesus) but it seems extremely like cheating if this incognito is not penetrated at all by human or historical discernment but simply by another act of God. One begins to feel that God is going through an elaborate and arbitrary series of conjuring tricks all of which He works unaided. It is not at all clear that this can be a fair representation of the relation between God and man, the pattern of which is to be perceived in and with the help of the Bible. I am inclined to believe that Barth is more concerned to preserve the godness of God than God is.

None the less, Barth is full of salutary warnings for all would-be debaters about God. He reminds us that if God is God then it will be necessary to let God be God if we are to know that God is God. The God of Theism is not determined by what is thinkable. He either determines what is thinkable or does not exist. This means that we have to take seriously the sheer givenness of claims to know Him and above all the sheer givenness of Jesus Christ and of the things connected with Him. Christianity and Biblical theism are not theories about the world arrived at theoretically and which account for everything, including Jesus. They are faithful approaches to the totality of things built up on the basis of a belief, however arrived at and however justified, that the tradition which finds its focus in Jesus is a source of true information about the ultimate shape and purpose of the life of man in the world. Belief in the reality of revelation is an essential part of the whole approach which has no *raison d'être* unless it is a source of newness—unless, that is, one is put in touch with sources of information and power which go beyond the information and power which is normally (i.e. apart from revelation) available to men. This inevitably involves the occurrence of particularity (some men aware, others unaware; some believers, other unbelievers and so on) to which the idea of Election especially draws attention. The theoretical offensiveness of this has to be set against the claimed matter of factness that the development none the less happens in this way. In any case, it is from this believed experience of newness, of information and resources that go beyond those normally available, that there have come the elements of judgment and gospel which have been the creative heart of the tradition of biblical theism. Men are judged by God and saved by God and thus taken far beyond themselves. Barth has taken these essential aspects of what believers in God have experientially and experimentally known to be involved in their coming up against God and has turned them into an account of all that is involved in knowledge of God and of all on which that knowledge could be based.

In doing this he so isolates Theology as not so much to make it incredible as to make it impossible for us to know whether it is incredible or not. But he also warns us that it is all too easy to make theology credible in a way which causes it to cease to be theology. A God in whom anyone found it easy to believe would be a particularly futile idol. The God of the Bible is certainly portrayed as existing in His own right. To believe in Him is to be changed. But it is by no means clear that there is the total discontinuity between belief and unbelief which Barth posits. If there is, then we can only wait for the miracle. But as we shall not believe in the possibility of such a miracle unless it has happened to us we shall not even wait. This seems an oddly hopeless position to be in in a world which God is both supposed to have created and to have been incarnate in. I shall conclude, therefore, that we cannot use Barth in the debate but that the debate continues.

[If it is wished to sample Barth directly I would suggest the three (brief) essays published by Collins under the title *The Humanity of God*. After that the going gets heavier. A possible way in might be to read *The Theology of Karl Barth—an Introduction*: H. Hartwell (Duckworth) and then use the Bibliography given there.]

Chapter Five

BRUNNER AND THE ENCOUNTER WITH TRUTH

WE ARE LOOKING for the 'whence' of data about God. We have seen that Bultmann maintains that there is no data about God but that one may experience such a transformation of one's own understanding of one's own existence that one becomes aware that this is the presence and salvation of God. This may be characterized as 'radical subjectivity'. It is centred upon oneself as an experiencing subject and it is radical as completely unsupported by outside evidence and yet completely self-authenticating. Barth, however, sets out a kindred but opposed position which may be described as 'radical objectivity'. God gives knowledge of Himself in, as, and through His Word to those whom He freely chooses by grace alone. This knowledge is given by sheer miracle. But as it *is* given it is objective. God's Word (Himself) is the Object of Faith. This is radical objectivity because, once again, it has nothing whatever to do with anything in the world and because the given godness of God is absolutely self-authenticating. Brunner basically agrees with Bultmann and Barth about the radicality of the Christian position. That is to say, he holds that Christian faith can be established and understood by revelation alone (and not by any substantial help from the world) and that faith is wholly and necessarily self-authenticating (for, as we shall see, faith is a personal encounter with the personal God). But he argues that positions both of subjectivity and of objectivity with regard to the question of God are quite wrong and mistaken. We must go beyond the categories of subject and object to the transcending one of 'personal encounter' or 'personal correspondence'. In working this out he believes that he retains the existential immediacy and warmth which, in his view, Barth has systematized away by his objective intellectualizing while he avoids the dissolving away of God into an aspect of our self-understanding which is the logical outcome, if not the actual meaning, of Bultmann's position. But he does not believe that he has worked out his position to counteract Bultmann or Barth (or even 'modern man'). He believes that it is the authentic biblical doctrine of the essential nature of truth—a doctrine which the Church obscured and forgot almost before the New Testament had finished being written, which was briefly rediscovered at the Reformation only to be rapidly re-obscured, and which is a direct challenge to the notion of truth prevailing at all times in Western civilization and dominant in the modern scientific world view.

Despite this very radical challenge of his to all world views on the basis of what he holds to be the biblical approach Brunner has always seemed to have much more sympathy with questions of ethics, culture and civilization in their own right than has Barth and he has written on them much more systematically and directly than Bultmann. Indeed, this side of his thought and approach has led him into a most bitter dispute with Barth, who has seen him as the most dangerous betrayer of the true Evangelical theology of the Word of God. (The most dangerous because he seems to take the Evangelical (Barthian) position but leaves the way wide open to the suggestion that both Revelation *and* our understanding of the world can lead to true knowledge of the true God. But this inevitably leads, so Barth holds, to putting knowledge of God at the mercy of knowledge of the world and God at the disposal of man—which is the supreme blasphemy and betrayal.) Brunner, of course, rejects these charges and we shall not pursue this particular matter here as he certainly rejects all natural theology in the traditional sense of the term, i.e. he does not believe that men can have any knowledge of God which they can know to be, or understand as, knowledge of God apart from the preaching of the Word (the world is in no sense a source of independent data about God). However, his acceptance of questions about ethics and culture as proper questions for theologians and not as entirely subordinated to the *one* question about the Word of God does, perhaps, make him somewhat less of a purely theologians' theologian than Barth and make some of his works at any rate of more easily general interest (cf. e.g. *The Divine Imperative* on Ethics). Whether this represents a fatal temporizing with the world on the part of a minister of the Word each debater must judge for himself.

Basically, however, for the modern debater about God the trouble with Brunner is exactly the same as that with Barth—a positivism about the Bible which it is exceedingly difficult to accept. Indeed, I should say myself that it is quite impossible to accept. But there both Barth and Brunner would agree with me. It is quite impossible to accept the Bible as the Word of God written unless and until one hears for oneself the Word of God. Then, together with or as part of the response of faith to the Word one is enabled, indeed compelled, to recognize the givenness of the Bible as the written Word in its totality. The Bible and faith are given together and inextricably. This is the practical and existential manifestation of the basic truth of the Reformation which is also the basic biblical and Christian truth—*sola gratia, sola scriptura*. God acts to kindle saving faith in us on the basis of grace alone from His end and of the Scriptures alone from our end and He has given the Scriptures for that precise purpose. Thus it is the Scriptures and not faith which provide the objective data about God. This is the correct Christian and Reformed reply to the situation which Schleiermacher diagnosed correctly but to which he succumbed through ill-advised subjectivism and enthusiastic pietism.

The true and biblical Christian must agree with the men of culture, of the modern world-view, that the world is to be seen as a wholly autonomous system. Religion resigns all claims on Science and Morality as far as knowledge of God goes. But Religion—or rather—Christianity which is not a religion, does not draw its data from faith as Schleiermacher supposed (and Bultmann supposes). Their account of the basis of Christianity being wholly and deliberately subjective can only lead to the dissolution of God into godly attitudes. Christianity draws its data from the Bible, a given criterion which, in its written givenness, is independent of the particular subjective reactions of any particular person or set of persons. But this givenness of the Bible is known only to faith and in faith. To the unbeliever there is and can be no criterion whatever which even begins to suggest that faith is anything other than a subjective attitude with no objective content. The believer, however, and the whole believing Church, must never succumb to subjectivism, that is to align oneself with the world. Rather, believers must submit themselves obediently to the objective givenness of the Bible, the written Word, so that the content, shape and direction of their faith, both indicatively and imperatively (what they should faithfully believe and how they should faithfully behave) may be determined by God's Word and not by their attitudes. In so far as it is true to say that 'the debate about God is really a confrontation between the undoubted givenness of that with which the scientist deals and—what?' (see pp. 19 and 22 above) then the Christian answer to the 'what?' is 'The Bible as the written Word of God known as such to those to whom the Word has given faith'. This, as we saw at the end of the last chapter (p. 81) leaves unbelievers waiting for a miracle, the possibility of which they cannot even conceive of and for which, therefore, they cannot consciously wait. But it is an answer.

I cannot myself believe that it is an answer which is either in accordance with the pattern of the Bible's portrayal of the relation between God, man and the world, or acceptable to any current understanding of man and the world. I suspect that pure miracle totally unrelated to any of the normal realities of the world is a concept which is as foreign to a truly biblical view of Creation as it is to any scientific approach to the world. The future of theism probably demands from the human end a greater recognition of mystery in the universe than some people in the mistaken name of Science are prepared to allow and a greater acceptance of the risk of faith than some people in the mistaken name of Theology are ready to admit. But if Theism has a future at all it is clear that it will be the divine end which must finally be decisive. Hence, insistence on the godness of God, on a Word of Revelation, on the sheer givenness of the experience of particular people and on the givenness of the records arising out of those experiences, and on a kindling of faith which gives conviction that past records point to present possibilities will all be necessary strands in any account of what is involved in knowing God. And in this matter of what is involved in knowing God, Brunner's concept of faith as encounter and truth as personal do seem of considerable importance for the whole debate.

In *Revelation and Reason* Brunner writes (p. 148), 'When the Christ of the Gospel according to John says "I am the truth" this is not a metaphor but a reversal of the usual rational idea of truth. God speaks, God imparts Himself; but behold, when God speaks it is no mere speech, it is not the use of language, but His "Word" is a Person, the Incarnate Word, God Himself present in a human person. He Himself—not something that can be grasped in words, something that can be thought, an idea in the mind—is the Truth.' Now, 'the usual rational idea of truth' is the one which leaves the endless problems of theory of knowledge with which philosophy has always been troubled. Truth is thought of as the proper correspondence between the subjective experience of the thinker and the objective reality of that which is being thought about with all the consequent difficulties about 'correspondence', 'reality' and the relation of subject and object. But the Bible's approach to truth transcends the whole subject-object dichotomy and reverses the notion of truth as the impersonal correctness of an idea relating the two. Truth arises, is experienced, is powerful, in personal fellowship when God gives Himself to man and man responds in faith. It is this personal correspondence which is truth, truth which fulfils the personality of him who knows the truth because he is opened to the personal reality of God. Thus 'I am the truth' is not a metaphor but a description. Christian faith is an encounter of the divine Self with the human self. Words lead up to this and words may be derived from this but words can neither contain nor get in the way of this personal encounter. Knowledge, faith and love become one and the same for personal correspondence is the interchange of self between person and person which is the essence of love (the self-giving love which is Christian *agape*, that is, and which is a possibility for man because God first loved us). Here all division between the persons related is overcome and the question which haunts the subject-object relationship (Is the idea of it correct, valid, true?) cannot arise. 'In the final analysis existence *in* love and knowledge *of* love are the same' (*Truth as Encounter*, p. 101). Hence, also, 'the true form of faith ... is not the so-called declaration of faith, the formulated Credo that has been learned, but prayer, even as the Word of God is not a formula to be believed but challenging, freely given address. The antithesis between object and subject, between "something true" and "knowledge of this truth" has disappeared and been replaced by the purely personal meeting between the God who speaks and the man who answers' (*Ib*. p. 117 f).

Here we have a powerful description of, and drawing out of, something which is central to the Christian faith as it has hitherto been experienced. Faith and love are bound together into prayer which passes into knowledge and knowledge which leads to prayer and the knowledge and prayer take form both as adoration of Him who is known and obedience to Him who is loved, and all in the understanding that it is He who first knows and first loves. This sort of personal data for the debate about God would seem to be both indispensable and yet ambiguous, because conclusive for the person involved and deceit for the non-involved. Yet when some participant in the debate about God declares authoritatively 'You cannot now believe in a personal God' all those who think they understand something of what Brunner is talking about will be bound to answer 'Oh, can't I!' and persist in their foolishness. Whether they ought then to go on and lay down the law about what is truth and what is not and about how the Word of God may illuminate our understanding of the world but that our understanding of the world may not illuminate our understanding of the Word of God seems to me to be quite another question.

[Anyone who wishes to follow up the absurdly brief remarks of the above chapter will find their way in through Brunner's *Truth as Encounter* referred to above. This is an English translation published by the S.C.M. press in 1964 of a book originally published in 1938, prefaced by a long introduction written in 1962, in which Brunner reflects on the present theological situation. Other books which reveal Brunner's standpoint and method are *The Mediator* and *The Divine Imperative* (both Lutterworth Press) and his *Dogmatics* (3 vols., Lutterworth Press).]

Chapter Six

TILLICH AND OUR ULTIMATE CONCERN

As 'ULTIMATE CONCERN', 'ground of our being' and 'the new being' are prominent phrases in much of the current debate and as the phrases come from Tillich it is to Tillich that we must now turn. None the less I must confess that I find Tillich considerably more debatable than God and that my guess is that his system will turn out to be unviable and his obscurities to conceal not profundity but muddle. On the other hand, it must be stressed that his sermons seem to many (at any rate to many Anglo-Saxons) to speak powerfully to their condition, that within his writings are many penetrating insights and that, of the theologians we are considering, he is the one who seems to be most sympathetically in touch with at least the aesthetic, cultural and psychological aspects of modern Western civilization. This is a paradox in itself as although he has this up-to-date and in-touch aspect, Tillich is philosophically the most old-fashioned of the current influences we are considering. (He has an underlying faith in the rationality of things in general which his strong dash of existentialism does nothing to negate. This aligns him with the philosophical tradition which assumes a necessary connection between Reason and the Cosmos and which found its culmination in Hegel. This becomes relevant when one considers the validity of his notion of 'ultimate concern' so we shall try and make this point clearer below.) In any case Tillich is clearly an important phenomenon. Whether he turns out to be a passing fashion or a lasting prophet only time can show.

Tillich is certainly deeply concerned with and relevant to one of the questions which we formulated as pointing up the debate about God viz.: 'What is that area of human experiencing in which awareness of God is to be found?' Tillich fully accepts Schleiermacher's discovery that such an area is not to be found in rational reflection on the world. That is to say, he agrees that reason, in the discursive sense, cannot put you on to God and that natural theology in the traditional sense is impossible. There is no direct argument from the world to God. On the other hand, Tillich says that he does not agree with Schleiermacher in supposing that you can find some general notion in the sphere of religion on which you can base the Christian understanding of God. It is no good, for example, analysing out the notion of absolute dependence and building your idea of God from there. But, again, Tillich cannot accept the insistence of such as Barth and Brunner that the way to the understanding of God is by revelation alone. Natural Theology is raising a right *question* when it asks what features of the world point towards God, and general philosophy of religion is likewise raising a right *question* when it asks what general religious concepts are relevant to the understanding of God. Indeed, Theology (exposition of the understanding of God) must have an apologetic concern, it must tie in with questions men are generally asking and with what men generally find thinkable. As Tillich himself puts it '(Theology) must answer the questions implied in the general human and the special historical situation.' (*Systematic Theology* I, p. 35). He therefore holds that we must look for our understanding of God by the 'method of correlation'. That is to say that we must put together questions men ask and the understanding of God already given in the Christian biblical tradition. When this happens in the individual, that is to say when I apprehend that the questions which I am asking and the Christian understanding of God fit together, then I have an existential awareness of God. All awareness of God, all theological understanding, must be existential and cannot be a rational, discursive, object-like awareness.

Tillich is thus aiming to take up an existential position while accepting Schleiermacher's complete dichotomy between Science and Religion and consequent denial of Natural Theology, together with at least part of the insistence of such as Barth and Brunner on the necessity of the givenness of revelation. He also claims to replace natural theology in its role of gaining a hearing for the Christian message by the questions which modern men find it thinkable to ask in their particular historical situations. This would seem to be an important and reasonable formulation of a Christian position for tackling the debate about God. Unless a message seems relevant to concerns which people already have, it can scarcely be listened to, and questions about its meaning, let alone its truth, cannot even arise. However, the formulation gives rise to considerable problems. Firstly, it may not be the case that people in fact ask the sort of questions to which the Christian message, properly interpreted, is the answer. Secondly, even if they do, it would not necessarily follow that because the Christian message answered these questions it was true. Thirdly, the answers one gets in any interrogation depend very much on the questions one puts. It might very well be, therefore, that the 'method of correlation' would distort the Christian message into a merely modern answer to modern questions, in which case the Christian message would be as relative as the particular questions it was addressed to. We would then have a sort of 'absolute relativism' which may be all that we can have but which would have abandoned any notion of givenness of Christianity.

To these objections I think Tillich would reply, firstly, that all men *do*, in their heart of hearts ask these existential questions, at least in so far as they are concerned to be human at all. (We shall consider what these questions are in a moment but it is straightaway worth noting that this answer which I am presuming

Tillich would or must give is in direct contradiction to the later Bonhoeffer who believes that man 'come of age' does *not* ask such questions. It is important to notice this in view of a tendency noticeable in the literature of the 'debate' to cite together short extracts from both Tillich and Bonhoeffer with insufficient attention to their context. I would myself suppose that both are right about some people some of the time and that they are both drawing attention to significant features of the climate of opinion. Neither, however, is really giving universally valid descriptions of how people do in fact behave. Rather, they are fixing on features present in the complexity of the human situation known to them which they *judge* to be most significant for approaching that situation. A wise debater will, therefore, never feel himself bound by what is declared to be 'thinkable', although he will be very stupid to ignore the insights of such as Tillich and Bonhoeffer.)

To the second objection (that a relevant answer to a real question is none the less not established by its relevance as a true answer) I suspect Tillich would have a two-fold answer. On the one hand he would admit, or even welcome, the objection if by 'true' one means 'objectively true'. In this 'sphere' of 'God' and of 'Ultimate Concern' one has gone beyond the subject–object approach which is proper to one's normal descriptive dealings with people and things and in which alone the concept of objective truth applies. So one does not *know* that one has a *true* answer to questions of ultimate concern. One is simply existentially aware that the ultimate questions are answered. This is very much akin to Bultmann's notion of awareness of 'authentic existence', only Tillich calls it experience of 'the New Being' (see below). Here Tillich is dealing in his own way with the problem of the transcendence or 'non-objectlikeness' of God which we discussed in the chapter on Schleiermacher (see esp. pp. 33 ff.). He is trying to describe the 'shape' of faith (what it is like to be a believer) but he is no more prepared than Schleiermacher or Bultmann to allow that faith is a basis for, or even has the nature of, *assertions*. That is to say that faith cannot be taken to be about anything in any sense akin to that in which knowledge is about something. This is so, both because we cannot have knowledge of anything outside the scope of scientific knowledge and because God, being 'beyond' cannot be, in any sense, the 'object' of knowledge. This is why Tillich's (justly famous) sermons are full of such things as exhortations to be aware that 'you are accepted'—passive verbs without any mention of the agent. To mention an agent would be to objectify God and this would in one sense go beyond the evidence (There is no object-like evidence for existence) and in another sense drag Him down to the level of objectlike existence where there can be no answer to the question of ultimate concern. But all this leaves us with the converse difficulty that if there cannot be said to be an agent, it is extremely difficult to see what meaning can be given to the notion of 'being accepted'. Perhaps faith has either got to go further (and make claims about existence) or else cease to exist.

But we must also note that Tillich has another side to his probable answer to the question about the connection between a relevant answer and a true answer. This is that Christian faith is a decision or recognition that the answer to our ultimate concern is to be found in and in connection with Jesus, that this recognition is self-authenticating and that it is or includes a kind of cognition (i.e. knowing) and that it is, therefore, Truth and known to be such. Moreover he insists that experience is not the *source* of the contents of the Christian understanding of God but the *medium* through which they are existentially received. We might translate this into our terms by saying that you require a godly attitude to be aware of God but that is not to say that 'God' is the name for your godly attitude, but for that to which your godly attitude is a response. But if this *is* so or is claimed to be so, ought he not to 'come clean' and admit talk about God in an object-like way, while taking full account of the difficulties? It is this almost systematic ambiguity in Tillich which causes some people to conclude that he is, at best, a pantheist and reduces God to an aspect of the universe, while others believe that he has translated the language of transcendent theism into the only viable form which modern thinking and a true appreciation of the otherness of God could find acceptable. If the former are right then it would seem that the third objection (that the method of correlation correlates the Christian method with modern questions simply by relativizing it) holds good. If the latter are right then the third objection is already answered. For myself, I cannot see how Tillich's language will work unless the transcendent God exists both transcendentally and in an object-like manner (i.e. He is 'there' to be the agent) but I can well see that Tillich's manner of talking may help many 'modern' men on to the 'wavelength' where the existence of God can be appreciated. Further, he is surely right in maintaining that the evidence which causes one to pass over from believing that there might be or from wishing that there could be a God, to assurance that there is and to commitment to Him, must lie in existential awareness (the experience, response, obedience, knowledge, of faith).

We must finally, however, consider the nature of these allegedly universal questions of ultimate concern. They boil down to the question of 'Being'. Why do I or does anything exist? And this is not a curiosity question but an anxiety question—a question forced upon us, at work deep within us, because of a variety of what Tillich calls 'limit' or 'boundary' questions. This is where we pick up Schleiermacher's notion of absolute dependence, transposed by Tillich from the romantic and enthusiastic calmness of the eighteenth and early nineteenth centuries into the neurotic and obsessive worry of the twentieth. Death, frustration, alienation, threats to identity, hostility of our fellows and to our fellows, and many other features of our imperfectly personal lives, bring us up against the limits of our current existence and force upon us the anxious and destructive question which is our ultimate concern 'Where is the ground and meaning of my existence? How can I be enabled to be myself?'

The answer to this question of Being which is our ultimate concern is the New Being in Jesus. Tillich says that 'the question arising out of this experience (of his situation by modern man) is not, as in the Reformation, the question of a merciful God and the forgiveness of sins; nor is it, as in the early Greek church, the question of finitude, of death and error; nor is it the question of the personal religious life or of the Christianization of culture and society. It is the question of a reality in which the self-estrangement of our existence is overcome, a reality of reconciliation and reunion, of creativity, meaning and hope. We shall call such a reality the 'New Being' ... (*Systematic Theology* I, p. 55). He goes on 'If the Christian message is understood as the message of the 'New Being', an answer is given to the question implied in our present situation and in every human situation. But this answer is not sufficient. It leads immediately to the further question, 'Where is this New Being manifest?' Systematic theology answers this question by saying: 'In Jesus Christ .... He who is the Christ is he who brings the new eon, the new reality. And it is the man Jesus who in a paradoxical assertion is called the Christ. Without this paradox the New Being would be an ideal, not a reality, and consequently not an answer to the question implied in our human situation.' (*Ib.* p. 56).

The last two sentences of the quotation tie up with Tillich's insistence that experience is the medium through which we understand God and not in itself the source of this understanding. Christian faith is not just experiencing 'New Being'. It is experiencing and even knowing the New Being as a real possibility, indeed an actuality, because of Jesus. In an age which tends to be dominated by psychological approaches to 'reality' this approach is clearly a very powerfully apologetic one. But if it is all that can be said with conviction or hope of some sort of truthfulness about the Christian message it becomes very dubious. For Tillich says frequently that Jesus is the Christ *because* he manifests or is the occasion of the manifestation of the New Being. Also he is very sceptical of placing any historical value on the gospels and insists that what matters is entirely our experience of the New Being in Jesus and not history in any sense or in any degree. For if history mattered, then our faith would, at least to some extent, depend on history and this is impossible for a matter of ultimate concern. (How could a *total* conviction or commitment depend on something historical which must, *ipso facto*, be only a *probability* more or less remote?)

This refusal to involve faith in the risks of historicity, combined with the deliberate choice of the question of Being and the reality of the New Being as the basis of our understanding and commendation of the Christian message means that it is a presupposition for accepting the Christian faith (and of the whole of Tillich's system) that the question of Being is a real question (universally asked and literally ultimate) and that it must have an answer. What we take for granted is that we all see a meaning in asking the question of being as *the* ultimate question which concerns us and that further this question has a universally valid answer which is the 'ground of our being'. But this is just the old-fashioned idealist assumption, that the Universe is rational, where 'rational' means that which satisfies the deepest and most valuable questions of the human spirit, to which we referred in the first paragraph of this chapter (p. 89). But many men who have 'come of age' in our modern scientific understanding of the Universe, of society, and of anthropology find it much more rational to hold that if there is 'anything' which is 'ultimate' it is equations about energy or whatever is the subject-matter of the equations and that our 'concerns' are nearly infinitely various, certainly not unifiable, and that they can receive only immediate and not 'ultimate' answers. I suspect that for all his apparent pessimism about the neurotic state of the human situation Tillich is basically an intellectualistic optimist who has never doubted that the human psyche in its depths vibrates to great questions to which there are great answers. It may well be no accident that it is to Anglo-Saxons that he has on the whole appealed hitherto and not to the Continent from which he comes, for neither Britain nor America have been emotionally conditioned by having absolute nothingness staring them in the face in the way in which many in Europe have. Thus neither Tillich nor many of his enthusiastic hearers seem to be existentially aware that the debate about God is often about whether Tillich's ultimate questions mean anything at all. On the other hand, there is also a failure to recognize (what Bonhoeffer came to stress) that the immediate possibilities and questions open to modern man are so many, so rich and so satisfying that for many people ultimate questions just do not arise and that to hanker after them is held to be an immature refusal to accept that immediate questions put us on to that which is truly valuable and that this valuableness is none the less valuable for being, inevitably, limited and 'non-ultimate'. We shall consider further how the debate stands with regard to what might be called the tough-minded, scientific, humanist in the next chapter.

Meanwhile, we may, perhaps agree that in the question about the ground and meaning of our existence, psychologically and existentially understood, there is a pointer to an area of human experiencing which may be a particularly powerful medium for awareness of God. But to attempt to erect a system of either theology or philosophy on this question seems to be a mistaken undertaking and to make particularly clear to us that the debate about God can be neither entered in to nor settled or lived with by any one set of considerations. Further, we may also be forced

D

to conclude that the nature of faith and the possibility of there being any meaning to the notion of 'ultimate concern' are more at risk than Tillich has reckoned with. Perhaps we have little ground for assuming that we have any ultimate concern until we share the conviction of the apostles that the historical Jesus is truly to be recognized both in history and beyond as the Christ of God, so that we have grounds in faith for looking to the God and Father of Jesus for the ground of our being and the fulfilment of our existence. But this means that faith has involved in it a definite element of historical judgment. Still, to the question 'Dare we tie up our ultimate concerns with particular historicalness?' we, in our particularity, may feel obliged to reply 'How dare we do anything else?'. We may find that the debate about God becomes focussed in the question 'Why risk belief in a God who takes historical risks?'

Dr. Tillich died on October 27, 1965.

[Those who wish to investigate Tillich for themselves should read the two collections of sermons viz.: *The Shaking of the Foundations* and *The New Being*, after which, if you are really going to give Tillich's system a chance to establish itself, you must tackle at least the first of the three volumes of his *Systematic Theology*, or read A. J. McKelway's excellent survey, *The Systematic Theology of Paul Tillich* (Lutterworth Press).]

Chapter Seven

BONHOEFFER AND THE MISTAKE OF LOOKING FOR DATA ABOUT GOD

BONHOEFFER IS A martyr of the Christian Faith in the old and original sense of that term, viz. one who witnessed to the reality of his faith in conditions of great stress, culminating in suffering and death. Thus he enters into the debate rather as a prophet who shocks and a witness who testifies than as a systematic thinker who contributes to structured and comprehensive answers. But it must be equally borne in mind that prior to the period of his 'martyrdom' Bonhoeffer was a very highly trained, highly skilled and highly subtle thinker and theologian. The prophetic, challenging and tantalizingly fragmentary theology of his last years emerges out of years of the discipline of the knowledge of God practised in the devout and original exploration of the Lutheran tradition, often under great personal and political stress and with many experiments in ways of Christian living appropriate to both the times and the message of the Christian faith.

In so far as in his last letters he was negative Bonhoeffer was negative on a very positive basis. It does no honour to his name and is entirely out of keeping with his life to suppose that 'religionless Christianity' has anything to do with the casting aside of strict spiritual discipline, frequent prayer and the most rigorous attention to the Christian and especially the Biblical tradition. A call to enter into the Cloud of Unknowing needs much positive preparation and a very exacting response. Without these the clouds will probably turn out to be those of ignorance, muddle and the slackness which looks for cheap grace, and have nothing to do with the cloud which hides the glory which hides God.

I believe that it is sufficiently clear that to the day of his death Bonhoeffer remained a convinced Lutheran, clear that the clue of our relationship with God was the *sola Fide* (by faith alone), that this faith was in Jesus Christ who is sufficiently and historically (and *not* mythically) shown to us in the Gospels and that behind Jesus and in Jesus stood God. In a letter of August 1944 (he was hanged in April 1945) Bonhoeffer writes: 'All that we rightly expect from God and pray for is to be found in Jesus Christ. The God of Jesus Christ has nothing to do with all that we, in our human way, think he can and ought to do. We must persevere in quiet meditation on the life, sayings, deeds, sufferings and death of Jesus in order to learn what God promises and what he fulfils. One thing is certain: we must always live close to the presence of God, for that is newness of life; and then nothing is impossible for all things are possible with God; . . . . all through we are sustained in a wondrous fellowship. To all this God in Jesus has given his Yea and his Amen, and that is the firm ground on which we stand. . . . the truth is if this earth was good enough for the Man Jesus Christ, if a man like him really lived in it, then, and only then, has life a meaning for us.' (see *Letters and Papers from Prison*, pp. 183 ff). Whatever Bonhoeffer meant by his call to Christians to be prepared to be 'without religion' it is clear that it was no call to be 'without God'.

Bonhoeffer agrees with Barth (and, indeed, with Schleiermacher) that the world is no source of data about God. For a good while he would seem to have been more or less satisfied with a form of Barth's theology of the Word wherein this Word both kindles faith and is received in faith and thereby supplies the independent data about God (*is* the data about God) which judges all other data. But the experiences of his war-time life seem to have built up in him a fresh approach to what we might call the world and ordinariness which developed all the force of a revelation. Barth's approach (and Bultmann's too) neglected the world. But this was not biblical. It was in the world that men lived, it was in the world that Jesus lived and the Bible portrayed the world as both created and redeemed. It might be true that the world offered no data about God but both the Bible and our common human condition demanded that it should be the world which we took seriously. Further, this was precisely what modern man who had now 'come of age' took for granted. This much misunderstood phrase of Bonhoeffer's is meant to draw attention to the fact that modern man has grown out of a certain sort of dependence. He is not dependent upon tales about a God or Gods to explain the workings of the Universe, he is not dependent upon miraculous and heavenly power to put right the evils of his life, (he sets to work with his sciences and technologies to right them himself) and he is not dependent on the promise of future bliss to make this life worth living, (as Bonhoeffer puts it: 'He has neither time nor inclination for thinking about his intellectual despair and regarding his modest share of happiness as a trial, a trouble or a disaster'. *Letters*—p. 147). Thus the so-called 'ultimate questions' —death, guilt, despair—do not generally arise at all and to try to make them do so is only fit for and successful with 'a small number of intellectuals, of degenerates, of people who regard themselves as the most important thing in the world and hence like looking after themselves' (*Letters*—p. 146). (Tillich, by implication here and by name a little later, is very severely handled.)

It is in this context that we can most easily see the point of Bonhoeffer's demand for religionlessness. He found himself forced to the conclusion that religion was seeking to maintain its foothold by exploiting men's weaknesses or by persuading him that he is weak where he is not. This is to put forward God as the God of the gaps which are to be found in man's meanness, weakness and despair. But such an approach is unworthy of God and of his creature, man. 'This is why I am so anxious that God should not be relegated to some last secret place, but that we should frankly recognize that the world and men have come of age, that we should not speak ill of man in his worldliness, but confront him with God at his strongest point, that we should give up all our clerical subterfuges, and our regarding of psychotherapy and existentialism as precursors of God. The importunity of these people is far too unaristocratic for the Word of God to ally with them' (*Letters*—p. 160). This would seem to be a splendid and justified protest against the so-largely prevalent religious policy and practice which turns God into a cosmic anodyne and makes religion the enemy, not the crown, of life.

Further, Bonhoeffer maintained, this religious way of carrying on proceeds from fear, the fear engendered by the collapse of the whole 'religious' situation. As he puts it, neither metaphysics nor inwardness any longer provides a religious premiss. Metaphysically, men no longer feel the need to fit the observed and observable universe into a framework *beyond* it. Psychologically and existentially, it is just blackmail to try and persuade men that they have some secret 'inwardness' where they can be clear about their need for a God who transcends their limits. Men are psychosomatic wholes who are to be understood and who, generally, understand themselves in a wider and more healthy context. (Bonhoeffer, in effect, accepts the position of what I called 'the tough-minded, scientific humanist'—cf. p. 97). Hence you cannot gain a hearing for Christianity by hooking it in to the gaps which men assume in the framework of the Universe or by latching it on to the needs which men feel in their understanding of themselves. The religious way of looking at the world which treats God as the *deus ex machina* at the boundaries of human understanding and experience is now nothing but a survival. Men have grown out of this and rightly so. Christians must grow out of it too and thereby allow themselves to be truly identified with Jesus.

'Myths of salvation arise from human experiences of the boundary situation. Christ takes hold of a man in the centre of his life.' 'We should find God in what we do know, not in what we don't; ... God cannot be used as a stop-gap. We must not wait until we are at the end of our tether; he must be found at the centre of life: in life, and not only in death; in health and vigour and not only in suffering; in activity, and not only in sin. The ground for this lies in the revelation of God in Christ. Christ is the centre of life and in no sense did he come to answer our unsolved problems' (*Letters*—pp. 154 & 142 f). As with all prophecy there is an absoluteness here which is proper to the urgency of the message but cannot be taken as a complete description either of the human situation or of the biblical understanding of things. None the less, Bonhoeffer is surely right to issue so strenuous a warning against the negativity of so much religion, against the fearfulness involved in looking for *special* data about God and against the religious tendency to rely on a spurious and external authority for the obedience and understanding of faith.

Jesus Christ *is* God's Word but he is not a Word who came or who comes with an external religious authority. He simply came and gave himself to men at the heart of *their* affairs, just as he comes and is to be found now 'in the midst' or at the centre of things. When he is so found he does completely transform a man's values (Shows him his godlessness, the sinfulness of his *strength* and creates newness of life) but he is so truly immanent, so truly a man, that there are no external or special aids to recognizing him, and so truly God who is truly transcendent that the newness of life is not the answer to current problems but real newness in the midst of the problems, which go on or not just as before in the world's own authenticity and autonomy. Thus there is, can be and ought to be no data other than the life of faith, lived out in love which is itself inextinguishable hope. But 'the firm ground on which we stand' is Jesus Christ.

Bonhoeffer's attack is on the Church's refusal to accept the situation about the knowledge of God in the world which we have found ourselves considering throughout. Where ought we really to take our stand about data about God, the experiencing of God, the status and autonomy of the world and of Science, and about the role of Jesus Christ? Like all original and creative challenges it is neither inclusive nor conclusive and becomes nonsense if taken as being the whole of the truth. But the attack on religion as relying on adventitious authorities (e.g. that people happen for a long while to find a God of the gaps thinkable) so that both God and the world can be kept at a distance and so that a religious way of life becomes a speciality of religious people would seem to be wholly salutary both for sane living (which cannot be based on a dichotomy but must be concerned with unity and wholeness) and for a faith which takes account of the biblical doctrines of Creation and Incarnation. Bonhoeffer attacks religion but he presupposes the existence of the Christian fellowship and the givenness of the Bible. He does not suppose that belief in God can lose its basis in the scandal of particularity but rather encourages believers to have the courage and assurance of their convictions and asks them not to be dismayed when they find that, as with Jesus, the only way of demonstrating the truthfulness of their faith lies in being faithful.

[It is in *Letters and Papers from Prison* that practically all the famous Bonhoeffer 'quotes' are to be found, but to give him a real chance to speak fully at least his *Ethics* (both SCM Press) ought to be dipped into. The essays in *The Place of Bonhoeffer*, edited by Martin E. Marty, are also most helpful and can conveniently put you on to his other works]

Chapter Eight

PERSONAL POSTSCRIPT—
THE CONTINUING DEBATE

As I SEE it, Bonhoeffer's attack on religion, the church and even Karl Barth for either neglecting the world or refusing to take it seriously brings us full circle from Schleiermacher.

The latter declared that religion resigned all claims on science and morality. He thus insisted on a complete divorce between the basis for our attitude to God and the basis for our attitude to the world. Bonhoeffer from the beginning found himself out of sympathy with Bultmann's attempt to deal with this admitted dichotomy by resting our relationship with God on sheer inwardness (the discovery of authentic existence as a personal possibility). He eventually found himself out of sympathy with Barth's attempt to deal with the same admitted dichotomy by resting our relationship with God on the sheer miracle of the objective self-giving of the Word. Everyone agreed that you could not directly relate religion and the world—with the exception of Tillich. In Bonhoeffer's view he fails miserably, both as a matter of fact (men do not, as a general rule, ask ultimate questions) and as a matter of morals and theology (Tillich's method is based on psychological blackmail and is a far too unaristocratic grubbing about in the meanness of men to be allied to the Word that created the world and was incarnate as a man). Hence the dichotomy of which Schleiermacher made a virtue must be ended. Modern man's approach to the world without childish dependence, the biblical concern with events and life in this world and the man

Jesus understood against the traditional christological understanding of him as 'God with us' all combine to make it clear
that the Christian way to end the dichotomy is to abolish religion
and accept the world. But you do this with unshakable faith in
Jesus Christ as God's Word who is to be found in the midst, at the
centre of things.

From any point of view which seeks to be in continuity with
the biblical and Christian approach to reality, Schleiermacher's
dichotomy must be a mistake. The biblical doctrine of Creation
and the Christian doctrine of Incarnation will not allow you to
make a complete separation between the basis of your approach
to God and the basis of your approach to the world. The doctrines
themselves may be myths but the logic of their mythology is
clear. God and the world are involved together (doubtless by
God's choice, but none the less involved for that—rather all the
more for that). Hence, if your approach to the world can in no
way be related to your approach to God, then it turns out that
the God of the Bible is not even a mythological characterization
of a true aspect of reality. He is simply a primitive mistake. Unless,
that is, it is possible to believe in Him *etsi non daretur* ('although
he is not given') as Bonhoeffer would say. But here I would myself think that Bonhoeffer has fallen back into the very dichotomy
which he has so rightly attacked and that in a more absolute way
than ever. He has identified an inevitable and important aspect of
faith with the full account which faith must give of itself.

In all the following ways Bonhoeffer seems to me to be right.
He is right to refuse to follow Schleiermacher, Bultmann, Barth
and Brunner in neglecting the world. He is right to refuse to
follow Bultmann, Barth, Brunner and Tillich when they refuse
to discuss or accept historicity and try to insist that all that matters
about Jesus is authentic impact or miraculous givenness now. The
tie-up between God and the world makes it inescapable that our
faith has a relation to historical probability and risk. It must be

at least reasonable to believe that Jesus did actually live in *that* way and did actually make *that* impact (sc. the way and the impact reported in the Gospels). It may be stupid of God to get involved in that way and perhaps it proves that He does not exist but, once again, the logic of the mythology seems alarmingly clear (and also encouragingly so. I do not think I would myself be interested in the debate if it were not about an involved God). Bonhoeffer is also right in refusing to follow Schleiermacher, Bultmann and Tillich in putting their whole stress on sheer inwardness. The logical end of existentialism is the Absurd, not 'being accepted'. And the retreat to inwardness in the face of the achievements of 'outwardness' as manifested in Science and Technology suggest immature withdrawal to womb-like depths rather than an approach to an authentic maturity, whether that is reached in the bleak heights of disillusionment, the glorious heights of fulfilment or the lesser vantage points from which one comes to terms with the discovery that life is worth living for as long as it is livable.

Finally, he is right to find no way of escape with Barth and Brunner into the unassailable authority of the given Word, unassailable because it is not only not related to anything else but also not to be recognized unless the recognition is miraculously granted. Sheer grace would seem to be sheer nonsense, not only in terms of logic but also in terms of the Bible wherein God appears to give man the chance and the responsibility of answering back. Again, no doubt, somewhat stupid of God and a blunder which may well prove that He does not exist, but I doubt if the position is helped when even such a theologian as Barth seeks to protect God from Himself. I would think, therefore, that Bonhoeffer is right in rejecting these various answers to the debate. Indeed, he is right to make it clear that there is, here and now, no answer to the debate. God is known in the debate, not as a means of stopping the debate.

But now that we have worked our way out of Schleiermacher's *dichotomy* I believe we must take up again Butler's *division* between reason and revelation in our approach both to the world and to God. But we may do this only if we heed all Bonhoeffer's challenges and do not seek to re-establish religious authority as a worldly authority. Reason will never establish that God exists. He is far too divine to be an object of reason. Revelation, stripped of the accidental historical and social prestige of the Church, must be understood as always having the form of the servant. Hence God will not be known in a way which will enable those who acknowledge Him to be sure of Him in a way which will enable them to make use of Him or to speak dominatingly or condescendingly of Him to others. Knowledge of God must have a form which is always open, humble and obedient to the world as well as to God who is involved in His world. But because He is so involved there will always be proper questions which can reasonably point in His direction. There will be healthy questions which arise out of the mystery, the strength, the possibilities of the world and of man in the world. And because man is not altogether healthy there will also be questions of the sort Bonhoeffer would have us reject, although in asking them we must certainly reject the gloating which so rightly appals him. They must be asked only with compassion and in the knowledge that they are asked of us, not of 'them'. And in these questions, both healthy and unhealthy, and about some of which we may well learn from Tillich, will be found many pointers which do tie God and the world together, if there is a God.

For the substantializing and existentializing of this 'if', we are dependent upon revelation—upon the historicity of Jesus Christ, the givenness of the Bible and the continuing witness and fellowship of the Church. Here we are directed to the givenness of the Word of which Barth speaks, of the encounter with living Truth which Brunner describes, and the authentic change of the very content of our living with which Bultmann is concerned. But we need to bring to bear the pointers which reason can give us upon the existential and experiential manner in which revelation largely impinges upon us. Only thus can we be reasonably clear that we are not just experiencing but also experimenting, that we are not developing godly attitudes but finding out about God. The role that is played in this experimental living by the corporate life and tradition of the Church is vital but would require another 'Guide' to itself (Liturgy, traditions of prayer, traditions of doctrine and of meditation, practices of worship and ways of life, the learning of the meaningful use of language from people who use it meaningfully, and so on and so on).

I would suggest, therefore, Butler and Bonhoeffer as primary guides to teach us the method by which we should live in the debate about God. And we may surely learn from the difficulties about believing in God which occasion the debate, or are discovered by the course of the debate, that very many of us believers in God have been shockingly forgetful of what is involved in the godness of God. Here the witness of Barth is particularly joined to the challenge of Bonhoeffer. I would argue that what the debate about God particularly shows us is not that God cannot be believed in but that in much at any rate of Western Christian theism He has as a matter of fact not been believed in. We have practised religious idolatry rather than the obedient and expectant worship of the living God.

Now that adventitious religious aids are being steadily removed so that even the religious cannot fail to recognize this, we shall see whether God can continue to maintain a people for Himself who are His people for the sake of Himself and therefore for obedient living in the world. At least we should no longer be surprised that the reasons which even the most skilful theologians and philosophers can give for believing are never adequate. He would not be God if they were.

We are back therefore to the position that either God does not exist or else He must establish His own existence. The believer is, in his heart of hearts, aware of this. For he knows that the debate is not about whether God exists but about how He can be shown to others or hung on to when doubt invades oneself. In reality there are no adequate reasons for God's existence. He is. The atheist also understands this. He does not believe.

INDEX